BY SEARCHING

BY SEARCHING

by

ISOBEL KUHN

LONDON
OVERSEAS MISSIONARY FELLOWSHIP

© OVERSEAS MISSIONARY FELLOWSHIP

First published	..	..	..	May 1957
Twenty-three reprints		..	..	1957–1967
Reprinted	..	..	..	January 1968
Reprinted	..	..	..	February 1969
Reprinted	..	..	..	.. April 1970
Reprinted	..	..	..	.. June 1971
Reprinted	..	..	..	August 1972
Reprinted	..	..	..	.. March 1974
Reprinted	..	..	..	December 1974

ISBN 85363 011 9 (paperback)
ISBN 85363 012 7 (casebound)

Made in Great Britain
Published by. Overseas Missionary Fellowship
Newington Green, London, N16 9QD
and printed by The Camelot Press Ltd,
Southampton

CONTENTS

ACKNOWLEDGMENTS

My thanks are due to Alma Smail for the generous and sacrificial use of her time and strength in typing the manuscript of this book.

ISOBEL KUHN

THE QUESTION THAT PIERCED THE MIST
"Canst thou *by searching* find out God?"—JOB 11:7

THE ANSWER
Ye shall *seek* me, and *find* me, when ye shall search for me with all your heart.—JER. 29:13

Jesus said unto him, *I am the way*, the truth, and the life; no man cometh unto the Father, but by me.—JOHN 14:6

Search the Scriptures . . . they are they which testify of me.—JOHN 5:39

If any man will do His will, he shall know of the doctrine, whether it be of God. . . .—JOHN 7:17

CHAPTER ONE

ON TO THE MISTY FLATS

To every man there openeth
A way and ways and a way.
And the high soul climbs the high way
And the low soul gropes the low
And in between on the misty flats
The rest drift to and fro.
But to every man there openeth
A high way and a low
And every man decideth the way his soul shall go.
JOHN OXENHAM

"OF course no one in this enlightened age believes any more in the myths of Genesis and . . ." But here Dr. Sedgewick paused in his lecture as if a second thought had occurred. With a twinkle in his eye, he said, "Well, maybe I had better test it out, before being so dogmatic." Facing the large freshman class, who were hanging on his words, and pulling his face into gravity, he asked: "Is there anyone here who believes there is a Heaven and a Hell? Who believes that the story of Genesis is true? Please raise your hand," and he waited.

Up went my hand as bravely as I could muster courage. I also looked around to see if I had a comrade in my stand. Only one other hand was up, in all that big group of perhaps a hundred students. Dr. Sedgewick smiled. Then as if sympathetic with our embarrassment, he conceded: "Oh, you just believe that because your papa and your mama told you so." He then proceeded with his lecture, assuming once for all, that no thinking human being believed the Bible any more.

Brought up in an earnest Presbyterian home (my grandfather was a Presbyterian minister and my father an ardent lay preacher) I had been carefully coached in the refutations of modernism before my parents had allowed me to enter the University. If it had been a case of arguing the claims of modernism *v.* fundamentalism, I do not think I would have been shattered in my faith. But there was no argument. There was just the pitying sneer, "Oh, you just believe that because your papa and your mama told you so," and then the confident assumption that no persons nowadays who thought for themselves, who were scientific in their approach to life, believed that old story any more.

On the way home from class I faced the charge honestly. *Why* did I believe the Bible? The Genesis explanation of life's origin? Why did I believe in Heaven and Hell?

It was because I had been taught it by my parents and church from the hour I could understand anything. Was that reason enough for accepting it? No, I agreed with Dr. Sedgewick that it was not a sufficient basis to build my life upon. We had experienced remarkable answers to prayer in our family life—didn't that prove the existence of God? But my psychology course taught that mind had a powerful effect over matter. If I had not been so gullible maybe I could have seen a natural explanation. Our twentieth century believed only when there was a test and a proof. We were scientific in our investigations; we did not swallow the superstitions of our ancestors just because they were handed to us.

Dr. Sedgewick, Professor of the English Department in our University, was an ardent follower of Matthew Arnold's "sweetness and light" philosophy, and of Thomas Hardy's materialism. Yet he was so apparently patient and kind toward us whom he felt were still bound by our parents' old-fashioned thinking that he won our affection and respect.

At the end of my walk home, I came to the conclusion that I would henceforth accept no theories of life which I had not proved personally. And, quite ignorant of where that attitude would lead me, I had unconsciously stepped off the High Way where man walks with his face lifted Godward and the pure, piney scents of the Heights call him upward, on to *the misty flats.* The in-between level place of easy-going; nothing very good attempted, yet nothing bad either; where men walk in the mist telling each other that no one can see these things clearly. The misty flats where the in-betweeners drift to and fro; life has no end but amusement and no purpose; where the herd drift with the strongest pull and there is no reason for opposing anything. Therefore they had a kind of peace and a mutual link which they call tolerance.

I did not know that I had stepped down to the misty flats. I just was conscious of a sudden pleasant freedom from old duties. If there was no God, why bother to go to church on Sunday, for instance? Why not use Sunday to catch up on sleep, so that one could dance half the night away several times during the week?

Again, if the Bible was but a record of myths and old-fashioned ideas, why read it every morning? That took time and it was much easier to sleep in till the very last moment, getting up just in time for the first class at Varsity. Prayer, too, became silly. Talking to someone who may be did not exist.

I would not call myself an atheist; because, well, there were those childhood answers to prayer still to be accounted for. But I called myself an agnostic—I frankly did not know if there was a God or not. It was a popular thing to be on the misty flats, you had plenty of company. And one was respected as being modern and intelligent to question the old faiths. Life drifted along so pleasantly—*for a while.*

My home training still had an effect upon me. Jesus Christ, now seen blurred in the mists which denied His godhead, is an acknowledged historical character. And His name was still as an ointment poured forth to me. He was like a perfume which haunts and calls so that one stops, lifts one's head and drinks it in wistfully. His name was the sweetest melody I knew and never failed to stir my heart, even though I had ceased to seek Him. His purity and holiness made me hate besmirching things.

And all this because my father and my mother had taught me so.

So when I broke with the old religious habits and frankly went into the world, I still was choosey in what I did. I never smoked. The tainted breath and stained fingers or teeth of the smoker revolted me. I told myself I was too dainty for such doings.

Neither did I drink. My father, broken-hearted at my callous turning-of-the-back on all my home training, still warned me as a medical man what drink could do to a girl.

"Drink affects men and women biologically, and under its influence girls can be led into sin that they would never consent to when in possession of their senses. Dr. Hall and I have such come into our own rooms all the time. They never meant to, but there they are. Keep away from liquors and you can keep yourself pure, perhaps." So I did not drink. Also I had *signed the pledge* when twelve years old, and a certain whimsical loyalty to my childhood self kept me from breaking it.

So amidst the gay group at the University I was considered *a good girl*, and even a Christian! But I knew myself: I wasn't.

In my studies I took the honours course in English Language and Literature which brought me much under the influence of Dr. Sedgewick. But in my extra-curriculars I was mostly interested in the Players Club, the amateur theatrical club of the University. Apparently I had a gift for acting comedy parts, and in my freshman year I won life-membership in the Players Club, not usually attained by a first-year student. The staff patron of our theatricals was Professor H. G. C. Wood, also a member of the English Faculty. He was a believer in God and Christ, and not an atheist like Dr. Sedgewick, and his friendship helped to keep me from extremes. But the theatre was his hobby and soon became mine. Urgently my mother pled with me to attend the Young Women's Christian Association. I went several times, but was frankly bored, so dropped it. I loved the theatre and I liked to dance and these occupied my spare time. In fact, our Varsity 1922 year book has, as comment opposite my picture: "And oh the tilt of her heels when she dances!" No shadow of the missionary there.

In my second year I was elected to be Secretary of the Students Council; at that time the highest position to which a woman student could be elected. I met the leading young people of the University and became secretly engaged to Ben, one of the star rugby and basketball players.

Ben was a returned soldier from World War I, several years older than I, not handsome, but six feet two or three in height. He came of a good Baptist family and my mother encouraged our friendship. He even took me to his church on Sunday nights! It made a nice inexpensive date, for Ben did not have much money and when he asked me to marry him said that our engagement must be kept secret lest his "old man" be angry with him for getting involved before he graduated. I insisted that my parents be told, but his never were. We went together for nearly two years, and my path was perceptibly down-grade.

CHAPTER TWO

SLIPPERY WAYS IN DARKNESS

Wherefore their way shall be unto them as slippery ways in the darkness: they shall be driven on, and fall therein: for I will bring evil upon them, even the year of their visitation, saith the Lord. JER. 23:12.

AFTER the stretched muscles of climbing, to find oneself on the level is very relaxing and pleasant. Therefore The Misty Flats are attractive to foot, eye and palate *at the beginning*. There is no hint that the pretty mist will gradually close in in darkness. There is no suggestion amid the gay chatter of the populous throng that there are slippery places, which are going to bring hurt. In the boasted freedom of drifting whither you will, there is certainly no sign that one is being *driven on*, as Jeremiah so shrewdly perceived was the reality. And above all, there is never a hint that the end of The Flats is the visitation of the Lord and the judgment of sin. Yet all that is the real truth.

In my senior year there came a day when my college chum, Cora, shook my foundations with a sentence or so. "Isobel," she said, "I think I should tell you something, even though it may hurt. Everybody but you knows that Ben is not loyal to you. He is taking Reba out behind your back."

I turned a stunned face upon her, and her eyes filled with tears of sympathy, but with true friendship she went on: "You remember when you were ill and could not go to his fraternity dance?"

"Yes," I replied. "He took Reba in my place that night; he asked me if I would mind and I said no."

"Well that was the beginning of it, I guess. They've been seen together a lot. People are talking and I can't bear that you should not know. I don't think he's worth breaking your heart over, Isobel," she said earnestly.

But it did break my heart. It was difficult to believe and yet I knew he had not been so attentive of late. My father had spoken to me about it. "You let Ben get too sure of you, Baby," he had said, using his tender pet name for me, the youngest in the family. "Show a man all the love you have *after you are married*, but keep it in reserve while you are just engaged. The elemental male *likes* to fight for a mate. What is the use of chasing a street-car after you've caught it?"

So it was not all Ben's fault. I had been inexperienced, I was still only in my teens. With the promise to be his wife I had truly given my heart to Ben and love struggled hard with "maybe if I . . ." and "perhaps I could still win him back." But it was Ben himself who made it hopeless.

I met him one morning at the entrance of the University; no one else was around, so I charged him with taking Reba out behind my back. I wanted to hear from his own lips that it was true, for love rebelled at believing it. He drew himself up to the full stature of his six feet two inches, and I never forgot the curl of his lip as he said, "Isobel, you're a softy. You don't suppose, do you, that after we are married, I'm not going to take other women out sometimes?"

"Then we part," I had whispered, dazed as if stricken. I was on my way home from a class and have never forgotten the dull agony of that walk. I knew I could never marry a man with such standards. That was the trouble. They were just the standards of The Misty Flats. But I had known the Christ and I could not be satisfied with less than the ideals He had set me.

So I found myself in the slippery places of darkness. Pride wounded me; love wounded me; sleep departed from me. I had signed up for the honours course in English Language and Literature, which in our university entailed more work than a mere pass degree. I was working hard and needed to rest during sleep hours, but I couldn't.

My mother was distressed that I should break with Ben and kept saying, "If you would only take my advice"; but I could not bear to discuss it with anyone. I discussed it with myself night and day. My father was my greatest comfort. He knew enough to be silent and just love me. He even sensed I was not sleeping. One night when all the house had been asleep for hours and I was still tossing, I heard him come into my bedroom. He knelt down beside me and prayed God to help me, but it only made me irritated. "Thanks, Dad," I said wearily, "I know you mean it well, but it doesn't go beyond the ceiling, you know," and I never forgot the groan with which he turned from my agnosticism and left the room.

The climax came just before Christmas. My birthday is December 17 and I was to be twenty years old, but I do not remember if it was before or after that date. The Post Office clock on Main Street had just struck 2 a.m. and I was still tense and tossing. I was desperate. I knew I'd be ill in the morning if I did not get to sleep. Then came the Tempter.

"Of what use is life?" he whispered. "Ben is only an average fellow. Probably all men are just like him. You'll never find anyone to love you like you want to be loved—your ideal is too high. And you'd never be happy with a lower ideal of marriage. Why go on with life? It has no purpose, only suffering. This would be a good time to slip out. There is that bottle in the bathroom marked *Poison*. A good long drink and your troubles are over." A good idea. The only sensible solution. I jumped out of bed and started for the bathroom. *Slippery ways in the darkness: they shall be driven on and fall therein.*

My hand was on the door knob when a deep groan, thrice repeated, broke the silence of the dark. It was my father, moaning in his sleep in the next room. I was not afraid, for I recognized father's tones, but I was startled into remembrance of him. I stood with my hand on the knob debating. If I committed suicide, Daddy would think I had gone to Hell. Of course, that would not make a place called Hell, but how terrible for Daddy to think so. He had been such a dear, kind father to me all my life. Dare I make him such a dastardly return? No, I couldn't be so mean and selfish. In agony I turned and sat down on the edge of my bed and faced the darkest moment of my life. I didn't want to live and I couldn't die! Oh the black despair of *The Misty Flats*. How little did I know of the golden sunshine pouring on the High Way above them. What a lot of heartache I might have been saved if I had only been told that God had already laid His hand on one who was to be dear husband to me, with the same ideals and the same passion for God's highest purposes.

But it was necessary that first I drink to the dregs the emptiness of the promises held out by The Misty Flats: only then could I be freed from their lure and subtle call.

And now a strange thing happened. That day I had been studying Matthew Arnold's essay on *The Study of Poetry*. (You remember, it was Sedgewick, a disciple of Arnold, who had first pushed me off the High Way?) In that essay he gives various quotations from the classics as touchstones of perfect poetry. One such was from Dante and ran: *In la sua volontade e nostra pace*. From my knowledge of Latin I had guessed the meaning: *In His will is our peace.* Now that sentence wrote itself across the dark of my bedroom. Dante believed in God. What if there were a God, after all? If so, I certainly had not been in His will. Maybe that was why I had no peace? An idea struck me. No one was watching to see if I were a fool or not. Sitting there on my bed's edge, I raised both hands heavenward. "God, if there be a God," I whispered, for I was not going to believe in what did not exist just to get a mental opiate, "if You will prove to me that You are, and if You will give me peace, I will give You my whole life. I'll do anything You ask me to do, go where You send me, obey You all my days." Then I climbed into bed and pulled the blankets over me.

CHAPTER THREE

WHAT YOU SHOULD NOT IMITATE

THE next thing I knew, it was morning and the golden sunshine of a December day in Vancouver was pouring into my bedroom. I lay there drowsily enjoying it when suddenly a thought startled me into full consciousness. I had been sleeping like a baby—how did it happen? Such deep relaxed slumber had not touched my pillow for many a long day. What brought it? Thought traced itself back to the experience of the night before. I had made a bargain with God. I had asked Him for peace and—*peace had come*. Oh yes, answered Reason; but that was easily explainable apart from God. That was no proof God existed. It was just the effect of mind over matter; I had committed my troubles to an imaginary being and that was why body and mind quietened down.

Restlessly I threw off the bedclothes and sat on the edge of my bed. I was not going to use religion as an opiate. I was going to be realistic or nothing; as a matter of fact, I believe I was born with "a flair for reality." But as I pondered the thought persisted, "You made a bargain last night. The Other Side kept His part . . . there was no stipulation as to how peace should come, *and it came.* Nobody knows about it and nobody shall know, if this should prove to be foolishness. Why not continue your part of the agreement and see?"

But what was *my part*? To yield my whole life IF He proved Himself. And in the meantime, why not try to seek Him?

Seek God? Where?

Can a man by searching find out God? Zophar had questioned Job, obviously not believing it possible. Job had tried to answer by pointing to God in His creative works. But the twentieth century had another theory for the origin of the earth.

Where does one go to search for God? Even as I asked myself that question, a picture from memory floated before me. It was at the Guelph conference of 1921 when the Student Christian Movement was formed. A young man was on his feet giving his testimony. "While I was interned in Germany as a prisoner of war," he said, "I got hold of a Bible and started to read it. *I found God through reading His Word.*"

I had been University delegate for the Y.W.C.A. to that convention, but had apparently been unaffected by it. I knew there was a conflict on between the modernist students and the fundamentalists—this young ex-soldier was earnest for the old beliefs. I was still an agnostic and weary of religious arguments. I let them talk and did not let it enter my heart. But this young fellow was aglow with something real: he was the outstanding memory of that conference to me, yet I did not even know his name. Now in my own hour of need I could see him standing there, radiant, affirming he had *found God.* And found Him through the Christ of the New Testament.

Well, I had a Bible. There it was on my bookshelf, unused, a bit dusty, but beautiful and new—a gift from my father when I graduated from High School. I pulled it down and looked at it. Modernists said the Pentateuch was not written by Moses; this was questioned, that was questioned. Was there anything that wasn't questioned? Yes . . . the historicity of Jesus Christ is beyond doubt. And the four Gospels are accepted as a more or less authentic record of His teachings. As authoritative as Plato's were of Socrates, at least.

So I decided to search for God *through Jesus Christ*; to read the Gospels only; to underline everything and anything that Jesus said *to do* and try honestly to do them. Also Jesus prayed, so I would begin to try praying again; cautiously, of course, and not really assuming that it went any higher than the ceiling. With that decided, I arose and dressed for another day's study at the University of British Columbia.

And now began a life at two levels. An outer level of study, worldly gaiety and pride, and an inner level of watching, seeking after God—if there was a God; always I added that.

God is not a puppet. Man may not pull strings and expect Him to perform—not even doctrinally correct strings, such as Balaam tried to pull. God is not man's servant, that a puny atheist may shout a challenge and He is bound to respond. Neither is God a genie, that if man is lucky enough to find the right combination of words, He will suddenly pop out and reveal Himself. God is our Creator; all powerful and dwelling in light unapproachable. He demands reverence. But He is also willing to be *Father* to such as come to Him by His ordained road, Jesus Christ; and as a Father He tenderly stoops to the immaturity of the babe in Christ. This is the only explanation I have to offer of the following facts. God answered prayers which were unworthy even to have been brought before His presence. If I prayed those same prayers today He would *not* answer them. He responded then, ignoring the selfish vanity of the request, simply because of the honest seeking at the base. He knew I meant it when I said I would give Him my whole life. *The Father seeketh such to worship Him—in spirit and in truth.*

For some three months after my "bargain" I experienced nothing convincing. I read the Gospels and prayed in private, but I never went to church or showed any outward interest in religion. Then one day I was invited to a private dance at the home of a girl friend, Jill. Jill had moved away to a different part of town and probably did not know that I had broken with Ben, but as she did not inquire as to whether I wanted him to be my partner, I had no opportunity to tell her. She usually gave a dance once a season and only invited Ben because he went with me, her friend. She usually just invited him and left it to him to arrange for my escort to and from her house. So as I prepared to go, I wondered if he would be there.

But on arrival he wasn't and I prepared to enjoy the evening thoroughly, for it was a small home dance with just our crowd, and I loved my friend dearly. Jill's new house was centre-halled, so that for dancing we had three spaces, parlour, hall and dining-room. I was dancing with Les (Cora's friend and long since her dear husband) when it happened. We had circled out into the hall when the doorbell rang. Jill opened the door and I beheld Ben, Reba with him, and he was ushering her into the house! I could hardly believe my eyes that he would have dared to do such a thing—it was like slapping my face publicly. And the dance was so small that there was no avoiding constant contact. I became completely unnerved. Trembling from head to foot, I began to walk all over Les's feet. Long hours of study, late hours of dancing, unhappy broken sleep had wrecked my nerves. I was undone; there was simply no escape from the humiliating fact. Les's look of respectful compassion did not help my chagrin. I could not fool Les as to the cause of my agony and the knowledge was too much for my pride.

"Les, I don't feel well—will you please excuse me?" and, stopping at the foot of the hall staircase, I fled up to the bedroom assigned as our dressing-room. Up and down the floor I paced in a rage at myself trying to use pride to whip my trembling body into control. It was perfectly useless—I shook like an aspen leaf.

Suddenly I remembered I was trying to prove if there was a God. With almost a sneer at such a ridiculous thing, I nevertheless prayed. "Oh God, if You are, please give me p——" but I did not have time to finish the sentence. Something like an electric current struck me, shot through me and I tingled all over. *It had come from above; and from outside me.* But it left me completely poised and quiet. Incredulous, I stretched out my hand—it was steady and firm. Without stopping to say "thank You," marvelling inwardly, I turned and ran down the stairs. That same dance number was still on and Les was still standing at the foot of the staircase where I had left him.

"I'm all right now, Les," I said gaily. "Let's finish," which we did. A wonderful exultation, a feeling as if I had new life pulsed through me and continued all evening. Ben asked for a dance and made no effort to conceal his admiration. "You are beautiful tonight," he whispered, but I gave an evasive answer. Our ideals were too different; I must not let affection get involved again.

The evening was a triumph of gratified pride and vanity for me. But when I was alone in my bedroom, emotional reaction set in. Ben was a superb dancer, and the longing to float through life in perfect rhythm together would not be challenged by common sense. Sleep again departed from me and I tossed in agony until morning.

But the one fact stood out. I had cried to God for help, my

lips twisted in sardonic unbelief that He even existed, but He had answered swiftly. This was no mind acting upon matter; the mind had had no faith at all. But help had come *from the outside entirely*. I was now convinced that Some Force outside me, intelligent, loving and powerful, was Up There trying to get in touch with me. Never again did I pray *if Thou art*. And now I wanted to know—how much could I ask of Him? Did He always answer prayer in Jesus' name? Morning and night I now prayed in faith. Those prayers were still all selfish and this is the part of my story where I do not want any young readers to try to imitate me.

Follow me in my pursuit of God—yes.

Like me, come to Him via the Christ of Calvary—yes.

Seek for the revelation of that Christ in the Bible—yes. But don't imitate my flounderings. I was pigheaded now in the matter of refusing all human advice, and my own level of living was so low that God could not meet me on a higher.

I wondered if God could answer seemingly impossible requests. For instance—get me invitations to certain balls and dances? It was our senior year and almost all our "gang" were paired off now, either engaged or going steady. There was no one who would be free to invite me, within the circle of my close acquaintances, unless I hinted—which I did not intend to do, ever. God answered wonderfully, causing my incredulity to marvel at *His power* to do it. I will just take space for one instance.

A neighbouring university had sent their football team to play ours and a *thé dansant* was to be given to the two teams after the match. It was purposely a small affair in honour of the teams, just the players and their girl friends and such team officers as the coach, manager, etc. Now Ben was one of the star players and I wanted to go; he had barged in on my party; now I wanted to go to this held in his honour to show that I was not dependent on him for a good time. A thoroughly low fleshly reason but also—it was hopeless to expect an invitation to such an exclusive party. Could God do it? I challenged Him.

The day before the match came. No one would ask me now —it would be an insult to ask a girl at such a late hour: sure proof she was only second or third choice.

That last afternoon a fellow student and I had arranged a rehearsal of a theatrical scene in which he and I were to act alone. George was a good friend of mine and engaged to a girl called Martha. He also happened to be on the manager's staff of the football team, but this I did not know then. He had come to my house for the rehearsal and after it was over and he reached for his hat to leave, he said, "Well, Isobel, see you at the *thé dansant* tomorrow afternoon after the match." Then I saw he did not know I had broken with Ben.

"No; I don't think you will, George," I said slowly.

He whirled around and shot me a keen look; then, gentleman that he was, he drew himself up and said with fine courtesy, "Isobel, last night Martha was called out of town unexpectedly. I thought I was going to have to 'go stag' to the *dansant*. May I have the pleasure of your company? I'll explain to Martha, I'm sure she won't mind."

It was just as simple as that. I was almost intoxicated with the wonder of it, and again the afternoon was a great triumph for me. I had more partners seeking me than there were dances, while Reba was more than once a "wallflower." In fact, while dancing with me, Ben had to excuse himself to go find her a partner!

Now, do I really believe that God was responsible for that? I am sure God gave it to me. Moreover, by piling on the triumphs He taught me a lesson I never forgot. I learned that pride and gratified vanity could never bring me peace or happiness. Underneath the gay triumphant surface I was miserable. My heart was often like lead even while my lips were chattering merry nonsense. This kind of a life would never satisfy me—I grew more and more unhappy and disillusioned. And that was what God wanted. It was as if He said, "If this is what you think you want, dear, have some more." And He stuffed the froth of life down me. Yet every time He got me an invitation when humanly speaking it seemed impossible, He proved to me again there was nothing He could not do for me.

All during this time, my parents knew nothing of my inward seekings. They sensed a change was going on, but I still refused to go to church with them and usually spent Sunday trying to catch up on the sleep I had lost at dances during the week! But there may have been a softening visible, for Mother began again to try to help me.

"Isobel, I want you to come with me to hear Professor Ellis. The meeting is just a Bible class, not held in a church, but in a classroom of the Vancouver Bible School. Just to please your mother. Won't you do a little thing like this to please me? I don't want to go alone."

And so I went.

I did not know that anyone else in that room knew me. In fact, I did not look at the audience; I had ceased to be interested in human beings. But the speaker held my attention. Professor Ellis was a very cultured, educated Christian gentleman. I liked his quiet, refined manner of speech. He was speaking that day on the Temptation of Christ, and as he went on to give his message, he also very frankly pointed out the liberal interpretation of that passage. Without any belligerent dogmatism, he courteously but deftly refuted their arguments. I saw clearly that here was a scholar who knew both sides of the argument. Here was a real gentleman who would never stoop to nasty remarks about an opponent. And, watching the quiet radiance of his face, I instinctively knew that here was a man who had *personal experience with God*. I decided that this was the preacher for me; I would come again.

Seated behind me was another Christian gentleman. White-haired, shy and reserved, he was known to me only as Mr. Wright, a friend of my father's. I forget if it was that first time I went to Professor Ellis's Bible class, or on a succeeding occasion, but at the close of the meeting he leaned forward and spoke to me.

"Isobel, I'm glad to see you here. I've been praying for you for some seven years," and his eyes flooded with tears.

I was stunned. It was about seven years since I had decided to dance and go in for worldly things against my father's pleadings. The yearning in Christ which lit up Mr. Wright's face stirred me to the depths, for my soul still knew periods of agony. With eyes as flooded as his own, I tried to murmur "Thank you," then escaped quickly from the building.

But every Sunday saw me back in that afternoon service, and weekly I was fed and nourished in the truth of God's Word. Professor Ellis's scholarship and his expositional preaching combined with his gentle culture had won my full confidence and I was willing to learn from him.

And so, my head still befogged by the Mists of The Flats, my Feet were once more planted on the High Way; prepared to climb, and my face steadfastly turned Godwards.

CHAPTER FOUR

MY YEAR IN ARABIA

I GRADUATED in May 1922, when I was twenty years of age. Because of my credits, I only needed to take five months' Normal School training in order to get a teacher's certificate. My ambition was to be a dean of women in some university and teach English. But as I was so young and inexperienced in teaching I had to accept an elementary grade school first.

I could have got a high school appointment up-country but my mother would not hear of it. She insisted I have a city school and so, being absolutely inexperienced, I had to accept a place as teacher of the Third Grade at the Cecil Rhodes School, Vancouver.

In the meantime my family had moved to Victoria, B.C. My father was roentenologist to Dr. Ernest Hall of Victoria, and mother sold our Vancouver home and purchased a chicken ranch just out of Victoria. This ranch was to be for my brother who had been a soldier in World War I and for whom employment must be found. He thought he would like ranch life.

So in February 1923 I found myself a "schoolmarm" in Vancouver and needing to find a boarding-house. For the first time in my life I would not live at home, but be "on my own," and receiving a monthly salary for which I need account to no one. The idea was distinctly pleasing. But where to board?

Somehow I ran into the mother of a girl with whom I had gone to Elementary School eight years before. They were a Scottish family, and the mother especially was a very superior person. Mrs. Hunter was a thinker, but, inbred with theosophy, had fallen in with the idea that it was wrong to spank a child. I have wondered if this was not the reason her children did more as they liked than she liked. The two youngest would not continue school, so had to take employment below their family cultural level. By the time I had my Arts degree, Mrs. Hunter was so reduced in circumstances that she was trying to run a boarding-house and asked if I would come to her. She was apologetic, for she had lost her best furniture and could not provide anything as comfortable as I had been accustomed to; but she was very clean, an excellent cook and her house was within walking distance of my school. My mother knew her and felt at ease that I should be with Mrs. Hunter, who was as loving and kind to me as if I were her own child.

So I found myself in this house—the only Christian. The two daughters were both engaged to sailors; the youngest child, a son, was a policeman and had a wife and small baby. The policeman's brother-in-law, whom we called Laurie, was attending Normal School, hoping to become a schoolteacher. As he was not yet earning, he paid but a minimum, if anything. This was the household among whom I became the ninth.

After graduation my particular clique scattered. Many went to other universities for further degrees. Some taught school, but went up-country, where they could get High School positions. In no time, I seemed to be alone and living in a different world. The young people of my boarding-house were very nice to me, but were all for the gay life—I did not care to join them. We had little in common but our boarding-house. Surrounded with young laughter and noise, I was as alone as if I had been in the deserts of Arabia. For a year and a half, God shut me up to that aloneness, so that I have always called it *my year in Arabia*.

A young fellow we will call Mac had begun to ask me out. He was still studying and asked me to the various big dances of the University from time to time, but as he did not live in Vancouver our dates were not frequent.

I had begun to attend evening lectures at the Vancouver Bible School, but it was just beginning and I do not remember meeting other Christian young people. I was lonely.

F. B. Meyer points out that this is one of the planned training schools of God. "One symptom of being on that path is loneliness." He continues:

Nothing strengthens us so much as isolation and transplantation . . . under the wholesome demand his soul will put forth all her native vigour

. . . it may not be necessary for us to withdraw from home and friends; but we shall have to withdraw our heart's deepest dependence from all earthly props and supports, if ever we are to learn what it is to trust simply and absolutely on the eternal God.[1]

For one thing I found it hard to keep my prayer times. The others in the house played cards and danced or had what they called a good time until long past midnight. I could not pray with those noises in my ears. To get up early for it was not productive either. Once up, my mind was rushing on to my schoolteaching, which, by the way, I was finding difficult. At last I hit on the plan of asking the Lord to wake me up around 2 a.m., when the house had settled to quiet, and then to arise for an hour's prayer and Bible study. This worked wonders. Always a sleepy-head, it was wonderful to me to be awakened each morning, as I was, and in the quiet of that still hour Christ became so real to me that often I felt I could have touched Him, if I but put out my hand. I was learning what Dr. A. W. Tozer calls "the awareness of His presence."[2] It satisfied me as nothing on earth had ever done. It filled me with a joy of communion that is inexpressible. It was in my *Arabia*, as I called it, that I learned fellowship with Christ, living person-to-person fellowship which henceforth became dearer than ought else in life to me.

The acute sense of His presence was not given during the first few months I was at the Hunter Boarding House. My head was still in The Misty Flats and my feet too entangled with the world. How I got lifted out into a clearer spiritual atmosphere is a story in itself, so I give it here.

It began with an angry disappointment.

But first I must explain that I was not happy teaching Third Grade (eight-year-olds). The children in my class fascinated me. It was my first real connection with children, for I was the baby of our family and we had early moved away from where small cousins lived. I was totally inexperienced with children and thought them "the cutest things." Even their little buttons of

[1] *Abraham*, by F. B. Meyer.
[2] *The Pursuit of God*, by A. W. Tozer.

noses fascinated me. Needless to say, I had discipline problems!
The small cherubs soon found out their teacher was a softy and
she was given daily samples of what unexpectedly naughty
things a cherub can think up—even without ever losing his
angelic smile!

Then the subjects I taught were so elementary—spelling,
arithmetic tables, simple nature studies and *drill*. Eight hours
each day one's delightful mental life must be tied down to such
boredom. I have often thought that if I had been allowed to
teach High School English I might never have become a missionary—I would have loved it.

But now I hated teaching. I found the discipline so perplex-
ing that I was afraid I was going to be a failure and became
thoroughly alarmed. This was to be my life-work! I decided I
must study teaching and so signed up for a Teachers' Convention
in Seattle during—was it Easter holidays? I've forgotten.

Now, in Seattle there was a boy-friend who had corresponded
with me since grade school, which we had attended together
(i.e. General Wolfe School, South Vancouver). I had not seen
Donald for years, but when I wrote that I was coming to
the Convention I got a letter right back saying I must stay at
his house and he would be at the boat to meet me. So it was
arranged.

I was just about to leave for the Seattle boat when a telegram
was handed me. It read: HAVE ARRANGED FOR YOU TO STAY AT
WHIPPLES', SEATTLE. LOVE. DADDY.

Was I annoyed! "Daddy, how perfectly mean of you. Oh,
when will you and Mother stop interfering with my plans and
realize that I am grown up?" Whipples'—who are they? Dim
memory finally produced vague outlines. "Oh religious friends
of Dad's. Yes; I remember now. So *that's* Dad's idea. Wants to
have them talk to me about my soul, eh? Well, they won't find
a porcupine more receptive. I'm just *not* going to be bossed like
this. I'll telegraph I've made other plans." But a glance at the
clock showed me I had no time if I were to catch the ship.
Thoroughly provoked I went aboard and to my cabin. By
morning we would be in Seattle.

Don was there all right and I explained my predicament

He was not put out. "Well, just sleep there," he suggested. "I can take you around from there," and so it was decided.

I don't remember anything of the Convention. I remember a nice supper with Don afterwards and an evening of fun—a dance perhaps. Anyway, I did not realize how late the hour was until we approached the Whipple house and found it in darkness. No; there was a dim light at the back. The door-bell ring produced other lights; then the door was opened by Mrs. Otis Whipple herself. Don was introduced, invited in, declined, said goodbye, and I found myself in the sitting-room alone with my hostess.

I do not know the kind of person I was looking for, but it certainly was not the kind I met. Motherly plumpness, a cheery voice, Southern warmth of hospitality, geniality and culture were what greeted me. Culture is a form of beauty; beauty of a trained mind, and a heart trained to think of the other person's feelings. Beauty of any kind has always had power over me and I was drawn to her immediately. Instinctively I knew she was not one to barge into my inner sanctum without an invitation; as yet I did not know that there are other ways of soul-winning!

God and my soul were never mentioned. Just a charming talk about my home; their old friendship with my father; of a girl, Tony Black, to whom I was supposed to bear striking likeness. She spoke of a summer conference at a place called the Firs; and of her husband's sister, a missionary in China recently widowed who was to be at the Firs this summer of 1923. More and more I relaxed; better and better I liked her. So finally when I was shown to my room my porcupine quills were all safely laid flat.

The next day was Sunday. I had resolved to bend to decorum enough to go to church in the morning, then I meant to claim the rest of the day to do what I liked. I had a girl-friend in the city and I had an appointment to spend the afternoon with her, Mamie. Idly I wondered that Mrs. Whipple had not as yet made any effort to get me alone and talk religiously. Little did I dream the truth, which she only told me years later. That first night, after we had all gone to bed, she could not sleep for the burden of *me*. As last she got up and went on her knees asking God the cause? For over an hour she battled in prayer that whatever was the reason He had sent me to them, it might be fulfilled before I left. Not before she felt she had prayed *through* did she go back to bed. Having committed the matter to the Lord, she did not get anxious as to how He would accomplish it: *she did not try to rush matters*, which in my case would have been fatal. One of her pet sayings was "Flexible in the hands of the Spirit," and she truly lived it.

The afternoon visit to Mamie was very pleasant (I had always loved her) until she asked me an unsettling question: "Isobel, do you like schoolteaching? Are you enjoying your work?"

"Oh, Mamie," I groaned in reply, "I'm not happy at all. All my life I've planned to teach, and now that I've graduated and am at it, I just feel like a misfit. And yes, I just hate it. If only I had got a High School position, I'm sure it would be different. I'm still sure I would enjoy teaching literature. But I'm only twenty-one, you know, and so could not expect to get right into a city High School, without any teaching experience. It's so inane teaching spelling and arithmetic. I just don't——"

"Isobel, I know what you need," struck in Mamie earnestly. "You need to see a phrenologist, and have your head read! He'd tell you what you are fitted for. And it just so happens that a very excellent phrenologist is in town, Dr. X——. He is a friend of ours and coming to supper with us tonight. His charge is very high, but as a friend of ours I'm sure he would do you for nothing. But you would have to come tonight, for he is leaving tomorrow."

"Oh, Mamie!" I cried, "How perfectly wonderful! There is only one snag. I'm staying with religious people, and they might be offended at a guest in their house going to see a phrenologist on *Sunday*. You know how particular some people are about keeping the Sabbath. Oh, if they will only consent! My hostess is really a dear and I just couldn't offend her. But I tell you—I'll go right back and ask her. If she says yes, I'll phone you and you make the appointment for me. Oh, it would be grand to be happy in one's work. It would be wonderful to know what one was fitted for in life."

"Well, Dr. X—— will know, I'm sure of that. All right.

Goodbye. I'll be looking for that phone call!" And we parted;
I to return to the Whipples' home with beating heart. Was I
about to lose the opportunity of my life because of old-fashioned
religious scruples!

Arriving back earlier than expected, I met Mrs. Whipple in
the hall, and went straight to the point:

"Mrs. Whipple, I would like to ask you a question. Would
you object to my going to a phrenologist tonight to have my
head read? I've not been very happy in my work and . . ."

"Well now, dear," she said in her cheery, comfortable way.
"let us go upstairs and discuss it. I'm not just quite sure I understand all that is involved. Here is Miss McCausland"—waylaying
another guest who was crossing the hall at that moment. "Miss
McCausland is a schoolteacher herself, and maybe she can help
us. Take her to the little front bedroom, Margaret. I'll be there
in a moment."

I did not learn until many years later why she delayed in
coming. But she ran for prayer help. Her young High School
daughter, Lois, was in the back of the house with two friends,
all of them just in their teens. It is interesting now to look back
at those three little maidens who were urged on to their knees
downstairs to intercede for the right direction of phrenologist-
seeker me upstairs. Lois later became Mrs. Nathan Walton of
the China Inland Mission. Evelyn Watson became her sister-in-
law, Mrs. Eldon Whipple, whilst the third young girl, Doris
Coffin, became Mrs. Willard Aldrich, author of the well-known
column, "Out of the Mixing Bowl."[1] But at this moment the
three teenagers were just told, "Isobel has come to a crisis in her
life! Pray her through whilst I go up and deal with her." So
down on their knees they went in prayer.

Upstairs Mrs. Whipple was saying to me, "Now, dear, tell
us everything from the beginning so we will understand."

So the flood-gates were unlocked and out poured the story of
my schoolteaching troubles and disappointments; I spoke freely
because I felt an atmosphere of loving sympathy, and sensed a
poise about these two women which seemed to say that *their*

[1] *The Moody Monthly*

lives were satisfying. So I unfolded this wonderful opportunity of having my head read by a skilled phrenologist, and the supposed snag—it was Sunday. With a beating heart, I looked up into that kind, wise and lovely face and said, "Would you object to my going on Sunday?" No tremor of horror or shock crossed her face at all; just a look of deep thoughtfulness as if she were weighing the matter carefully. Then came her answer:

"Isobel dear, I don't think the matter of its being Sunday is the important thing. It's like this: *God has a plan for your life.* The Bible says that He has created us unto good works and *foreordained* that we should walk in them (Eph. 2:10). That means He has foreordained a useful life for you, and He does so for each of His creatures. The point as I see it is—to find out God's plan for your life and then follow it. If it is His will to reveal that plan through a phrenologist, going on Sunday would do no harm. But if it were not His will to reveal His plan through a phrenologist, *going any day of the week would be wrong.*"

I was struck with the common sense and logic of her words and thrilled through and through to hear that God had a plan for my life. Daughter of an elder in the Church and granddaughter of a Presbyterian minister, I do not remember anyone ever telling me that before. I always had thought that God was a kindly, fatherly Being. Away off in the heavens somewhere we could call upon Him in trouble, but for the rest it was up to us to map out our own lives in good, honest work. Then we could ask His blessing and help from time to time. But that God was so minutely interested in *me*, that He would take the trouble to plan a career for me—plan it without my asking—the tender intimacy of a Love which could do that, just touched me to the breaking point. Hardly able to control my voice, I asked, "Well, how are we to find out His plan for us?"

By this time I was kneeling at the bed on which Miss Mc-Causland sat, Mrs. Whipple in a chair beside me. She reached for her Bible and opened it in front of me saying, "Isobel, I've always found His will *through His Word*, this Book. His plan for us will always be in accordance with the Scriptures. And with me, it usually is from the Bible itself that I get my leading." At that moment the telephone rang and Mrs. Whipple was called.

C

"Excuse me a moment, I'll be right back," she said. "Miss McCausland, will you tell Isobel what you think?" I do not remember what dear Miss McCausland said for I was thinking, "God's plan for my life is in that Book." Impulsively, I pulled it toward me. It fell shut and I reopened it at random with my eyes on Miss McCausland. Inwardly I was wondering what the Bible said about phrenology, when my eye happened to fall on the open page and there, unconsciously, my left hand lay with forefinger pointing at a verse. I read: "KEEP THEE FAR FROM A FALSE MATTER" (Ex. 23:7). It was as if a Voice had spoken to me and I was so startled at the directness of the answer to my inward question which no one had heard that my distressed heart collapsed with relief. I was weeping when Mrs. Whipple re-entered the room; weeping terribly, simply rent with sobs.

"It is all right, Isobel," she tried to say. "He'll lead you."

"Oh He has," I cried. "Look at this verse," and I pointed to *Keep thee far from a false matter*. She too marvelled at such a quick, thoroughly complete answer. But the piled-up heartaches of a whole year and a half of SEARCHING after God had reached a climax, and I could only sob until exhausted. Very tenderly and lovingly the two ladies ministered to me. Dear Mrs. Whipple never tried to pry; the privacy of the human soul was respected by her, and that was another reason we all loved and trusted her so.

I do not remember anything more of that visit, except that Mrs. Whipple told me again of The Firs Bible Conference and urged me to attend that July as her guest. I was not interested. I still shrank from evangelistic meetings with their worked-up emotion and high-pressure methods. I did not intend to be high-pressured into anything.

"Thank you, Mrs. Whipple," I said. "But I have already signed up to attend Teachers' Summer School in Victoria. Until God leads differently, I must earn my living and can only do it by teaching." And so we parted.

The Lord now wished to direct my thoughts into a channel where they would never have run of themselves. My life was about to turn a new corner, and strange to say, it all hinged at first, upon a pair of shoes. But that is the subject of the next chapter.

CHAPTER FIVE

A PAIR OF SHOES AND THE FIRS CONFERENCE

"HERE, Julia," said Mrs. Tom Cole to her sister-in-law, Mrs. Otis Whipple. "The Firs Conference will soon open and you need a pair of shoes"—with a significant look at her—and she held out a five-dollar bill. I do not know if those were her exact words, but the gift was given for shoes and a significant look along with it, as Mrs. Cole told me herself years later.

Julia Whipple was not one to neglect her personal appearance; in fact, to be well-groomed had been her lifelong habit, but of late funds had not been too plentiful. The story of how Julia and Otis Whipple gave their last earthly possession to the Lord, i.e. this honeymoon cabin at the Firs on Lake Whatcom, Bellingham in the State of Washington; and of how God used it to establish the yearly Lake Whatcom Bible and Missionary Conference which has been so blessed to themselves, has been told by Doris Coffin Aldrich in a book called *The Firs of the Lord.* Suffice it to say 1923 was to be only their second attempt at a conference, and Julia Whipple was hostess. What would others think of her shabby shoes? But she had something else on her mind.

She had been praying that Isobel Miller would come to the Firs (as we liked to nickname the conference). She saw, as I had not, that here was one groping blindly toward God, and open to dangerous misleadings if not carefully grounded in the Word. As is a young person's weakness, I might be carried off my feet by some magnetic personality of one of the many "isms," if I chanced to meet such, at this stage. I needed grounding in the Scriptures and I needed Christian fellowship. I had had a small college debt to pay back and had only been earning a salary for six months—maybe money would be a factor in bringing me. At any rate, she waved the matter of new shoes aside, sat down and wrote me a letter urging me to come, and saying that the enclosed five dollars, she felt, was the Lord's provision for my boat tickets. Once I reached the Firs I was to be her guest—room and board would cost me nothing. Wouldn't I come?

I received it quite casually, not at all impressed with any desire to go. It was Mrs. Whipple's kind heart, I told myself, and I was now forced to do something about it. But I felt my alibi would be easy. The conference came right in the middle of the summer school I had signed up for, I must get credit for this summer's study, and they would hardly give me full credit for six weeks' work if I ran off in the middle for ten or eleven days? So I made this my test, *and I prayed about it.*

"Lord, if it be Thy will I go, move the authorities to grant consent without reducing my credits, and I'll take it as Thy sign I am to go."

So the next morning found me before the Registrar of the Teachers' Summer Institute.

"I have been called to Bellingham on a matter important to me and I would like to apply for ten days' absence without reducing my credits. Could that be done, sir?"

He inquired my name, turned over a book, pursed his lips a moment, then said, "All right, Miss Miller. Just tell us when you leave and when you will return."

I could not believe my ears. Just the day before a fellow student teacher had applied for only a week off and been flatly refused! I still do not know how to explain it, but my full credits were given to me.

I came out of the office walking as if in a dream. I inquired the boat schedule and sent word to Mrs. Whipple that I was coming, how and when, and went home to pack my suitcase.

So it came about that one evening in July 1923 my boat arrived at Bellingham Pier. I had never been there before and knew no one, but as I looked eagerly around for Mrs. Whipple, a smiling young man and a sweet-faced girl stepped up to me.

"Isobel Miller? We've come to meet you. Eldon Whipple and Evelyn Watson—do you remember meeting us in Seattle? We've got a car here. Hop in! We have to drive to the conference ground, but it is not too far."

Their warm friendliness made me feel at home immediately and soon we were whirling out over curving roads with fragrant woods on either hand. It was a twisting labyrinth to me, but finally we turned into a path, drew up among tall fir trees and there was dear Mrs. Whipple coming to meet me. Her radiance, rippling laugh of joy, and overflowing hospitality were something to cuddle down into. I was duly hugged and kissed, then shown into a big fire-lit room. Older people sat on chairs, and the younger ones on the floor before the big, crackling open fireplace of logs. The flames threw a golden light over all faces, and the young people pulled me down on the floor to sit with them while the evening devotional service continued. Always shy and reticent with strangers, I was soon at home and filled with a wonderful content. The atmosphere was charged with the presence of the One whom I was learning to know and adore, and He was the centre of everyone else's attention too.

In the doorway I had been introduced to "my sister-in-law, Mrs. Edna Whipple Gish, whose story I told you in Seattle. She is to be your cabin-mate." Years afterward I asked Mrs. Whipple if this had been a premeditated arrangement, for it was to have a lasting effect on my life.

"I can't remember that it was," she said simply. "Edna's was the only cabin with a spare space, as I remember it."

After camp-fire service Edna led me through a woodsy path to the little cabin in the woods where she and I were to live. We slept together, but before going to sleep she pulled out a little worn Bible from beneath her pillow and read a chapter with me, prayed, then at "Lights out" we settled down with the perfume of the fir trees soothing us into slumber.

I had just time to think back over Edna's story before losing consciousness.

"This is Ellis's Bible," she had said to me as she reverently took the worn much-marked volume from beneath the pillow. Then I had remembered what Mrs. Whipple had told me in Seattle.

Edna met Ellis when he was on his first furlough, and found in him her ideal. He was a young man of deep devotion and consecration, and together they went to China to the South Gate section of Nanking city.

The next year they went for their vacation to beautiful Kuling, a famous mountain resort, where there is a pool and good swimming, also many lovely walks.

One morning they had decided on a swim—both were expert swimmers. As they left their tent they heard a cry from the pool. Ellis immediately ran and dived in to the rescue—a young missionary had caught a cramp and gone down. He was successful and saved her life, but he himself disappeared. Then Edna dived in to search for Ellis. As time dragged on and she could not find him, one can imagine the terror and anguish of her feelings. Theirs had been an ideal and wonderful union. Diving, searching, she did not notice that her body was being bruised and battered against rocks. Ellis—that was all she thought of. Finally, she saw his body washed up behind a little waterfall. Again she dived, reached him, dragged his body with her and got it to shore. But life had gone.

Exhausted she sank on a tree stump and covered her face with her hands.

A few minutes later she happened to look up and saw some Chinese coolies standing terrified with the dead man before them. Quickly she approached them and explained that the body on the ground was not her Ellis—that he was safe with God; and she preached Christ to them.

Edna's own body had taken such a severe beating that she was sent to the hospital and later advised to take a short furlough. Ellis's insurance money was enough to bring her to the Firs for the summer, and the Conference Council had asked her to lead the young people's meetings. We never knew what it was costing her to set aside her daily heart-break and be our cheery, radiant Bible teacher. Years later Mrs. Whipple told me how she would go to the Council and tell them she could not continue, but they would promise to pray for her, and back she would come to us.

She laid before us the Scriptural challenge to a consecrated life and to missionary service. I had never given the foreign field one thought up to that time. I was a very stay-at-home body by disposition and a veritable slave to physical comforts. Travel never attracted me, for it meant strange faces and strange ways—in other words, discomfort. Edna was the first to show me that I ought to be willing to give this up, if He asked me. When finally she gave a challenge to those who would surrender for foreign service, if He called, I put my hand up. I was surprised at how thrilled she was. To me it was a matter of course. That night I had made my bargain with God: I had promised Him my life. If He asked for it on the foreign field—why, of course, then I must go to the foreign field. It was not a question if I wanted to go. *I was no longer my own.* But then I had no clear indication it *was* the foreign field He wanted. I was willing, if it were, that was all. Why were they all so excited that I had raised my hand?

A much deeper blessing Edna had unwittingly brought me. Cabin life with her was my first encounter with a Spirit-filled life living in its daily routine habits. It was Edna *off the platform* who wrought most for me.

She sought the Lord's face before that of anyone else's at the beginning of each day. There was no wake-up chatter and pillow-flinging nonsense at dawn. This deeply bruised heart hungered and panted after the Lord, and her first waking thought was a longing for His fellowship and presence. And she kindled the same hunger in me. Remember, I had a bruised heart, too.

She read Philippians with me and Ellis's marginal notes.

"This one thing I do"—how it smote home because it was lived before my eyes. It got marked in my Bible, too.

"Rejoice always"—Edna had attained to that. How could I ever? I marked it, but decided to try for Phil. 4:11 as perhaps more within the possibility of attainment: *"For I have learned in whatsoever state I am, therewith to be content."* This became my life-verse for the next ten years or so.

"That I might know Him, and the power of His resurrection, and the fellowship of His sufferings, being made conformable unto His death" (Phil. 3:10). Great words that moved me to the depths of my being—they got marked down in my Bible. I was on that quest! But little did I know beyond that mere fact that my feet were on the High Way; I was in pursuit of Him.

And every man decideth
Which way his soul shall go.

To such will come direction; there will come introductions to others of His family; there will come many helps which only One, on the outside of us (meaning a force which is not of us ourselves), could manipulate; and always He will also be within us for fellowship and love.

CHAPTER SIX

EXTINGUISHED TAPERS

Who extinguishes their taper
Till they hail the rising sun?
Who discards the garb of winter
Till the summer has begun?

ANON.

AND now it will astonish some adult readers (and perhaps make them shake their heads dubiously) to learn that all this time I was still indulging in theatres, dances and worldly things. My father had long years before urged me to separate myself from these amusements, but my mother felt he was "narrow" in his views on such matters, and she felt they did no harm if discriminately chosen. So I had gone with her viewpoint as the easier and more pleasant.

Occasionally I had wondered about it, but had always fallen back on that old taunt, "You do this, or believe this, because your papa told you so." I was not going to give up any habit just because some human being told me to! If *God* told me to stop them I would obey; otherwise, I continued as I had been. These amusements were like the *taper* of our verse. They formed the light moments of my life—my *fun* as we Americans term it. I wasn't going to give up any *fun* just because some old religious fogey was prejudiced against it!

The first taper that I extinguished was card-playing. In Hunter's boarding house the young folk often played until past midnight, and if they had the wherewithal they put up some small stakes. I suppose the sailors thought a game inane that did not have the element of gain or loss to stimulate them. Of course, they called me in to play with them. I hesitated— more from reluctance to waste time and my precious pennies than for any other reason.

"Maybe Isobel doesn't think she should play cards, as she is religious," offered Jack gravely. Jack was one of the sailors, but very open to counsel. He even asked me to teach him the Bible at one time, and I believe he would have accepted the Lord if his wife and the others had not pulled him away. I grabbed this offer of a legitimate excuse in order to get out of such invitations easily.

"Well, to tell the truth, Jack, I would prefer not to," I answered.

"Then we're not going to tease her into it," Jack informed everybody. "You play the piano for us, Isobel! We'd like some music while we play."

So it ended up. I loved to play the piano and I loved to play hymns better than anything else. Those young folk did not object to my religious selections, so the strange anomaly took place night after night. They played and gambled whilst I played from my hymn-book. Of course, this left me free to retire to bed as early as I liked and the arrangement pleased me well. But, having "given up" card-playing, supposedly for religious reasons, I must in consistency hold to it on other occasions. So I just did. It cost me nothing. I always thought cards were a tiresome waste of good mental energy—they acquired nothing for you but amusement, and I did not find them very amusing. So out went the taper of card-playing.

It was during the summer of 1923, perhaps before I went to the Firs, that I had to extinguish a second taper. This was quite a different affair and one of which no human being had ever spoken to me. I was a voracious reader of romantic fiction. Novels just held me and were my favourite mental escape from my trials and difficulties, or from an evening which had to be spent alone. With a good love story I was immediately transported into another world, and if the drama was exciting I could not put the book down.

We were living with my brother on his ranch for the summer, and as there were no young people around I had to occupy many evenings, so a good novel was my first resort. This particular time, it was an exciting one and I could not lay it down. I might say that I never read the modern sexy novel; these were just clean, exciting love stories; but, like such, very often not really true to life. Life does contain moments of adventure, but they are interspersed with long periods of plain, unvarnished hard work. The real things of life are attained at these monotonous level periods, so to speak, more than they are at the high peaks of excitement. So that novel-readers who feed on the lurid and melodramatic are not prepared for the long stretches of routine work which fill every life. I believe this is partly responsible for the many broken marriages we have today. Young people think married life should be all moonlight and thrills and they baulk when they find themselves on the level stretches of plain, ordinary working together, which actually are the real life and backbone of a home.

Anyway, I was deep in the excitement of my book. Midnight came and I was so near the end I could not stop. In fact, it was one o'clock in the morning before I finished the book and took up my Bible for evening devotions. But I got no blessing from it. Never had the Bible seemed so drab and dull; and when I tried to pray later, the Lord seemed far away. "It's just sleepiness," I told myself, and curled up for slumber.

But the next morning was little better. God still seemed far away and the Bible stuffy and uninteresting. Before the Teachers' Summer Institute opened I was clerking in a Bible Depot, which belonged to my father. It was a sideline with him, as his real work was roentenology, but he had felt that Victoria lacked a good Bible store where reliable Christian books could be obtained as well as the Scriptures, and so he, supported by Christian friends, had opened this Bible Depot. I substituted for the clerk while she was on summer vacation, so I had to be in to the city by opening time. I went in by bus and had time to think. What had happened to me that the Lord seemed no longer real to me? And the Bible, which I had begun to read through from Genesis to Revelation for the first time in my life, had become insipid? I was alarmed. Sitting in the bus, I talked to the Lord about it in my heart.

"Oh Lord, what is wrong with me? Why can't I sense Your

Presence now as I have lately? Why has the Bible become dry?"
It seemed to me that He answered thus:

"When a child fills its stomach with ice-cream and soda-water, why does it lose its appetite for meat and potatoes?"

"Lord, do You mean the novel did that to me?"

"It excited all the fleshly part of your nature, didn't it? Did it do *anything* to help the spiritual?"

"Nothing, Lord. It kept me up so late. I'm tired this morning. Lord, if I promise to give up novel-reading, will You come back to me? Will the Bible come alive to me again?"

"Try it and see."

From that moment on, the Lord was real and present once more and the Word took on new meaning. My spiritual growth could have been traced by the markings in that Bible as I read it from cover to cover. I "discovered" verses that seemed to spring out of the page as His voice to my need at the moment. Unfortunately, that particular Bible was amongst our books which the Communists ordered to be burned, but one verse I remember was given me as particularly mine and, as such, I have claimed it through the years and it has been fulfilled to me:

Isa. 54:10: For the mountains shall depart and the hills be removed; but my kindness shall not depart from thee, neither shall the *covenant of my peace* be removed, saith the Lord that hath mercy on thee.

I need not say that the taper of novel-reading (which included magazine short stories) was extinguished from that day on. For about fifteen years I never permitted myself to read a love story. After that, when I had to be alone in Lisuland so often, with such problems pressing upon me, I used to read a bit at mealtimes; but they were, in the main, the old classics, such as Dickens, Thackeray, Brontë and Barrie. These I had read before so they had no "hold" on me to continue reading past mealtime, and they did give me a wholesome mental holiday for an hour, lifting me out of the canyon-world back into life among my own race.

Did I find it a hard denial?

*Who extinguishes their taper
Till they hail the rising sun?*

Does one begrudge candle-light when morning sunshine is pouring in the window? I was *richly repaid* for this self-discipline.

The next taper that the Lord touched was my dancing. Mac continued to invite me to the university big dances, and to some of the smaller ones occasionally. It was at one of the latter (was it a fraternity dance? I forget) that I ran into Marion A—— in the dressing-room. Marion was a Christian girl in our year who had abstained all through her course from worldly amusements. We had both graduated now and here we met at a dance!

"Why, Marion!" I exclaimed in surprise.

"Well, you are to blame, Isobel Miller," she said with her merry frankness. "You're the reason I am here tonight. You are a Christian too, aren't you? And all through our four years you danced and had a good time and I got left out of everything. People say you are a good Christian, but you dance, so I decided to dance, too. This is my first dance."

I did not know at the moment, but it was my last. I do not know how Marion ended up; but I fear she drifted from the Lord.

Back in the dancing-hall, I had as partner, for one memorable dance, a tall, good-looking boy whom I had known since High School days. His name was Keith and he was a science major. As we were waltzing around he made some contemptuous remark about "old-fashioned fogies who believe in God." Ah, said I to myself, here is my chance to witness. I always felt if I kept in with the dancing crowd, it would afford me contacts for Christ with people who could not be contacted otherwise. So I started in eagerly, "Keith, why do you say that? I believe in God, and you used to."

"Oh, that was before I met Dr. Sedgewick or studied science," he replied impatiently. "No one with a scientific approach to life believes that old stuff any more."

"Oh, but they do!" I cried eagerly. "I have been investigating God and have indubitable proof that He is!"

"What proof?" he scoffed. Then I tried to tell him, but he refused to believe. He got angry and we were arguing together hotly when a ripple of laughter brought us to ourselves. The orchestra had taken their seats. Just Keith and I were left; and we, unconscious that the number had ended, were waltzing round and round in the centre of the room obviously fighting over something.

"Better give up, Keith!" called out a pal from the side-lines. "A woman convinced against her will is of the same opinion still! They never give in and they don't know how to reason!"

When Keith saw what a laughing-stock we had made of ourselves he swore angrily, marched me to a seat and stalked off in high dudgeon. If there is one thing a man can't forgive, it is a wound to his pride; a public humiliation I had caused him and he "cut me dead" from that hour. My testimony to him had not only been a failure; it had left him more antagonistic than ever.

It was a very subdued and thoughtful Isobel whom Mac saw home that night. Was this the Lord speaking to me? I had led Marion A—— astray. I had further antagonized Keith. Was dancing worth it?

A few nights later Mac telephoned me and asked me to the Agricultural Ball—in April, I think it was to be. "Mac, I'm not sure," I parried. "That is so far ahead. Phone me a little later, will you?" and we left it at that. I'd need to pray about it before going to another dance. Was this just an accident or was the Lord speaking to me about giving up the dance?

I was in the throes of indecision when something lovely happened. The telephone rang one evening and a cheery voice with a rippling laugh called me from the other end. "Guess who is speaking, Isobel!" Only one person had such a contagious, delightful approach.

"Mrs. Whipple!" I cried in joy, almost trying to jump into the receiver. "Are you in town? Can I get to see you?"

"That you may," was the answer. "We are here on some business for just a day or two and we are staying with Mrs. Ernest Walsh. Can you come out, or shall we come to you?"

Hunter's boarding-house was no place for quiet discussion. "Oh, I'll come to you," I cried. "Tell me how to get there." Inside of one hour I was in the parlour of Mrs. Walsh's nice home, and seated on a stool at Mrs. Whipple's feet. Oh, it was the most wonderful feeling just to be near her again. Mr. Whipple was one with her, but a shy silent disposition which took time and experience to appreciate. However, she often appealed to him for his opinion and it was always worth waiting for.

"Well, tell me what you have been doing since Conference," she said gaily.

"That is just what I want to do," I answered. "For I have a pressing problem. Just before you called, a boy-friend phoned to ask me to the Aggie Dance (Agricultural students' ball), and I put him off but told him I'd tell him definitely a little later. I'm all in a stew about it," and then I told her of my adventure with Keith ——. She probably was scandalized to see that the girl she thought had been led into full consecration was still deep in worldly amusements *but she never showed it.* To have looked shocked at my doings would have made me resentful—for wasn't I *honestly* seeking the Lord and His will? I was merely refusing to act on *Your papa and your mama told you so.*

She did give a significant glance at her husband, then answered me so sweetly:

"I can quite see that you are in a mess, Isobel. You are trying to serve two masters at one time and it always has painful results. Let's see what the Word of God says. I Cor. 6:12: 'All things are lawful unto me, *but all things are not expedient.*' You are compromising and that is fatal *whatever realm it occurs in.* Have you ever told Mac that you have become a Christian?"

"Oh, no," answered this product of the twentieth century "Our set doesn't do that. It is a point of honour among us not to thrust our religious opinions upon the other fellow. I've never told anyone! It is my private life with God."

Poor Mrs. Whipple. What a warped little human being to try and straighten out! But she was *full of faith and of the Holy Ghost.*

"Those are standards of your old life, Isobel," she said gently. "2 Cor. 5:17 says that if any man be in Christ he is a new creature: *old things are passed away*: behold all things are become new."

Oh, what a lovely verse—down it was marked in my Bible. Why, it sounded as if it had been written just about me.

"But look at 2 Cor. 6:14-17, Isobel," went on my dear spiritual mother, " 'Be ye not unequally yoked together with unbelievers. . . . What communion hath light with darkness? . . . *Wherefore come out from among them and be ye separate*, saith the Lord.' That is the basis of our separation from things of the world and standards of the world. 1 Pet. 3:15 says that we should *be ready always* to give . . . *a reason of the hope that is in you*. I think it is your duty, under the standards of your new life with God, that you tell your friends about Christ and what He has done for you. You will be surprised at the spiritual blessing it will bring."

"But I did try to tell Keith," I wailed, simply terrified at this idea of witnessing.

"But look at the place you were in when you told him. You stood in the place of compromise and worldliness and then expected him to respect your testimony. No wonder he despised it. But now if you take your stand against dancing as belonging to your old life, but unsuitable to the new, I believe you will find Mac will have a different reaction."

"Well, I'll try," I said dully. Young people always think that the older folk don't understand their generation. Inwardly I felt this way at that moment and dreaded speaking plainly to Mac. He had been so fine to me; I shrank from offending him or rendering myself odious in his eyes as I had rendered myself in Keith's.

For the rest we had a pleasant time together and then I had to return home.

All the next day I dreaded that evening phone call, and when the moment came I went cold all over and was nearly paralysed with fright. But I gritted my teeth and took up the receiver. It was Mac all right.

"Well, Isobel," he said. "What is the decision about the Aggie Ball?"

My throat was so dry I could hardly get my voice out.

"Mac," I answered, "I hope you will forgive me. But I have become a Christian lately and have decided to give up dancing altogether. I do not criticize the gang in this matter, but I have had some experiences which make me feel that God would not have me continue to dance. I'm so sorry not to have told you before—I was just undecided."

A long silence at the other end, during which my heart beat so violently I was afraid he could hear it. I was trembling from head to foot. At length Mac's voice came over the wire:

"Thank you, Isobel, for being so straightforward with me. I honour you for not playing with me about this. May I have the pleasure of your company to the Baccalaureate Service on Sunday instead?"

"Oh, thank you, Mac! Yes, indeed. I would be delighted to go with you."

"It's a date, then. I'll call for you at nine-thirty. Goodbye."

I staggered to my room and fell across my bed in the weakness of relief. Mrs. Whipple had been right after all. Mac said he *honoured* me for being straightforward! And to prove it he had asked for another date immediately! Oh, how good of the Lord to let it happen that way. How did Mrs. Whipple know? She knew the general principles of life; that compromise wins respect from no one, but a straightforward testimony does. Clean-cut action does, too. The older generation may not understand all the new scientific terms of the young generation, but they knew the principles of life which never change. And it is a wise youngster who will not discard her or his *inheritance of wisdom and experience* from those who have gone before.

So the taper of dancing was extinguished, and forgotten very quickly as the Rising Sun flooded my life with new and fascinating interests.

There remained but the one taper, the theatre. I had only gone to good movies, an occasional opera (one of the classic

D

ones) or wholesome family theatre acts. There could be no harm in such? And they taught one much of human nature.

The last one I went to was a sweet, harmless story; I think it was *Smilin' Thro'*. I enjoyed it very much, but as I went home, once more all the old longings for romance and story-book experiences flooded me. The music too, had stirred up the emotional side of me and once more prayer was a blank and the Bible had lost its savour. In vain I tried to push through to the Lord's presence. "*My Beloved had withdrawn Himself and was gone*" then was true of me as of the little bride. "*I sought Him but I could not find Him: I called Him, but He gave me no answer.*" Song of Solomon 5:6. Later when I read the Song of Songs and came to this incident, I knew what it meant perfectly. I had been there myself—this, for the second time.

"Oh, Lord," I prayed, "if You will but return to me I will never go to the theatre again. You may have that also."

It was but a little that . . . I found Him whom my soul loveth: I held Him and would not let Him go.

Nothing was worth the loss of *fellowship* with Him. Then did the Sun of Righteousness arise in my heart with healing in His wings.

I remember only once being tempted to relight this last taper. Remember how alone I was, how young, how so accustomed to lots of friends my own age. It was an evening, perhaps in May, when everything in youth was calling for companionship and fun. The Hunter young folk were all going out together to see a movie and I would be left alone in the house.

"Oh, come on, Isobel," they teased, catching me by the hand. "It's a good clean movie tonight—can't possibly do you any harm. What does a young girl like you want to mope in the house for on such a lovely evening? Be companionable—come on with us!" They were a kind-hearted bunch and I was sorely tempted to go. The perfumed May air called to me from the open doorway. I was about to yield when I saw a doubtful look in Jack's eyes.

"Don't press her to do what she doesn't feel is right," he said quietly. That settled it.

"No, thank you," I returned. "Have a good time!" and

waved them gaily off; then turned to go upstairs with a heavy heart. I entered my bedroom, drab, rather dark, with its cheap furniture, and cried out into the silence of the empty house, "Oh, Lord, is it to be so dull always? And I'm still young? A girl looks her nicest at twenty-one or two. Nobody to go with! Nothing to do but Bible study! Oh Lord, speak to me!" and I pulled over my Bible and opened it at random.

The words on the page sprang up before me. John 6:67: *Then said Jesus unto the twelve, Will ye also go away? Then Simon Peter answered him, Lord, to whom shall we go? Thou hast the words of eternal life.*

I sat there reading and re-reading that quiet potent question. He did not refuse to let me go back to my earthly tapers. He just wanted me to think well before I did. Did I really prefer them? Would I change places with any one of the three girls who had just left the home? God forbid—I shrank from such a thought. Did I want to go back to Ben's world of loose loyalties? Again I shuddered. *Lord, to whom shall we go?* There was no other road. The low road? Not for a moment. The Misty Flats? God deliver me from ever again drifting around there. Then there only remained The High Way.

"Forgive me, Lord," I bowed my head in contrition. "There is no one I want but Thee. Please comfort me." Then the sense of His Presence so filled the room that it is too sacred to talk about. Suffice it to say, I never again looked back; but more and more I learned the value of communion alone with Himself. Dr. Tozer has pointed out how our generation is in danger of missing this sacred joy. He says: "We have been trying to apply machine-age methods to our relations with God ... our thought habits are those of the scientist not those of the worshipper. We are more likely to explain than to adore." *Searching* is a scientific procedure, but we want to beware that it does not get into mechanical ruts. "We read our chapter, have our short devotions and rush away, hoping to make up for our deep inward bankruptcy by attending another gospel meeting, or listening to another thrilling story told by a religious adventurer lately returned from afar."

We need to worship and to adore as well as to analyse and

explain. Mary of Bethany learned much by just sitting at His feet, listening to Him and loving Him. Our generation's greatest lack is just here.

By now the summer of 1924 had begun. Unknown to me, my year in Arabia was over. Mac had gone out of the city on a summer job. When he returned I was in Chicago at the Moody Bible Institute. We have never seen one another since. My Rising Sun had planned many things to fill the place of my extinguished tapers, but each was to be a separate and delightful discovery. Next on God's programme for me, was a contact which changed the whole course of my life.

CHAPTER SEVEN

J. O. FRASER OF LISULAND

I FORGOT to say that when Mrs. Whipple lent me a book called *The Growth of a Soul*, at the close of the Firs Conference, 1923, she had no idea that for many years Dr. and Mrs. Isaac Page had been secretly praying that God would lay His hand on Isobel Miller for missionary service in China. She just rejoiced that in the life-story of Hudson Taylor, founder of the China Inland Mission, were experiences of searching for God and proving Him, which were parallel to some which were now mine.

Anyone who knows *The Growth of a Soul* will recognize the gold mine it was to me. Hudson Taylor went much deeper in his searchings, of course, and came out with definite maxims for life and conduct. "Learn to move man, through God, by prayer alone" was one of the many that I eagerly noted down, and it had blessed me all my life. By the time I had finished the book one thing was clear to me. I wanted to belong to the mission Hudson Taylor founded: I wanted to work with the group who daily proved God in that quiet, unostentatious fashion. Having finished. *The Growth of a Soul*, I went on to read the second volume, *The Growth of a Work of God*—the founding of the China Inland Mission. It was while reading this that I received a call to the field. Previously I had felt a call to the *Mission* regardless where it worked. But as I read of the sorrows and sufferings of Chinese women my heart was greatly stirred. I knew now what heartache was. But when I was groping for a way out, my Bible was on my bookshelf. It was easy for me to find the way. But what about those who had never heard of Christ? No matter how willing they would be to follow Him fully if they only knew of Him, and His death for their salvation, they must perish unless someone went to them and told them. *How shall they believe in Him of whom they have not heard? And how shall they hear without a preacher?* Romans 10:14. I knew I must go and tell them.

So when I arrived at the Firs Conference, 1924, my decision to apply to the China Inland Mission had already been formed. Needless to say, no one needed to give up a pair of shoes to bring me to conference for the second time! I had saved up, during the year, and had also applied for the position of waitress to earn my board while there.

I was simply thrilled to be back at the beloved place. I ran, almost flew, from spot to spot of hallowed memory. The cabin which Edna Gish (now back in China) and I had shared; the spot in among the tall fir trees where I had often prayed alone; the open-air auditorium where our classes had met; the original Firs cabin with the big fireplace where we had had such blessed times of testimony—I wanted to see them all. The cabin was the last in my inspection tour and I dashed in eagerly and was halfway to the centre of the room before I could check my impulsive entrance. For it was not empty. One lone occupant, a middle-aged gentleman, was sitting there by himself; he smiled at my surprise, and I tried to apologize whilst backing out as speedily as I could.

"Some old bachelor," I told myself, and flew off to look at the kitchen. How I knew he was unmarried, I do not know. Maybe it was a certain lonely, wistful look in his eyes. Anyway, I promptly forgot him in the joy of greeting other arrivals, and getting into the swing of the waitress routine, which was new to me. Little did I dream that I had just met one who was to be a lodestar spiritually to me and to the dear husband God was planning to give me, but of whose existence I, as yet, knew nothing.

It was not until the evening meeting when to my intense surprise I found that the "old bachelor" of the sitting-room loneliness was seated on the platform, and being introduced as our principal speaker for the conference! Mr. J. O. Fraser of the China Inland Mission, was his name. I had never heard of him, and apparently neither had anyone else. Even Mr. Whipple probably did not know at this point that this young Englishman was an honours graduate of London University in electrical engineering, and a brilliant pianist. He appeared among us as a simple missionary, and never by word or action gave any hint of his extraordinary gifts.

When he got up to speak, he told us simply how the C.I.M. had sent him to one of the furthest corners of China, to the border of Burma and Yunnan Province. There he worked among the Chinese for several years, but had frequently noticed a people coming into the market who were not Chinese at all. They did not speak Chinese among themselves and they did not dress like Chinese. Their costume was very colourful (especially the women's) and trimmed with cowrie shells and silver bangles. Also they wore turbans. They knew some trade-language Chinese and through this he discovered that they were the Lisu tribespeople who lived in the mountains of the Salween River canyon. They had never heard of the Lord Jesus Christ, and their language had never been reduced to writing—they were entirely illiterate. Moreover, they were not idol-worshippers, like the Chinese, but animists who worship demons directly. God called him to go to these people with the gospel; and since he had several evening hours at his disposal, Mr. Fraser decided to divide up his work among the Lisu, taking a different phase each evening. For instance, one night he took us itinerating over those wonderful alpine mountains, climbing great heights to where small villages perched (precariously it often seemed!) at the edge of abysmal ravines. Another lecture he gave up to the language difficulties; how he learned it from living with them in their smoky little shacks; how he reduced it to writing; and how with two colleagues he was led to form what is now called the Fraser Script.

Another evening he gave over to the patience needed in teaching the older folk, illiterate from their youth. He was full of humour and his descriptions of the old ladies who declared they had no power of memory, and then were tricked by him into relating with detail what had happened to their children fifteen years ago, were simply hilarious—and touching. We learned to love those old women.

Another lecture was on the spiritual battle in the heavenlies. How he had roughed it, and laboured, and given them a written language and still there were so few converts and such as did come were not stable. Then he wrote his mother in England to gather in the neighbours and *pray*. It was only after this prayer group began to function in earnest that "the break" came in the Lisu tribe. At the same time he on the field had been led to resist in Christ's name the devil and his host who were holding this tribe enchained. As I sat listening I saw plainly that it was true the *Lisu church was born in prayer travail*, and I decided that I must employ this weapon of "all-prayer" too. It is attainable to any of us; it is obviously so effective. I received a life-pattern at that moment for which I have ever been grateful.

Another evening was given over to the joys of harvest. He took us on a trip with him, and his descriptions were so vivid we were simply transported out of America to the mountainous banks of the Salween canyon. We saw him (dressed in the costume of a Chinese coolie, lest better clothes distract attention from his message!) and a Lisu carrier or guide, climbing the steep approach to one of these high villages. He cupped his hands to his mouth and gave the Lisu call. "*Ma-pa chi la-o!*" (the male teacher is arriving!) at which all the dogs of the village rush out and down the path at them.

> Hark, hark the dogs do bark
> The ma-pa are coming to town!

Then the banging of doors and the shouts as the brightly coloured costumes of the women flashed back and forth and the men folk darted forward to drive off the dogs. The Christians line up to shake hands, and as the tall missionary goes down the line each woman has managed to stick an egg into his hand as she gave the welcome handshake! They had learned that he liked eggs! So he always had to carry a bag over his shoulder to hold the eggs (fresh and ancient!) which such a visit collected!

He told of the Prophet's Chamber behind the chapel, which the Christian villagers built for him, learning that queerest trait of the white man; that he liked privacy sometimes! Just imagine *wanting* to be alone! Eh, eh, how queer. Perhaps it came from the colour of his skin: but if he wanted it he should have it. So he had a little Prophet's Chamber of his own in each village.

Then would start the catechizing for baptism. He told of going to call the next candidate and finding the man on his face, prostrate in prayer, asking his new Saviour to help him to answer correctly, so that he might be adjudged ready for this solemn step. And so on. The last night he said he needed more missionaries—young men of consecration willing for the privations and loneliness such a life entailed.

Down in my seat in the side aisle my heart thrilled with love for the Lisu people. Inwardly I prayed. "Lord, I'd be willing to go. Only I'm not a man." Never did the vision of the Lisu tribe leave me. I dared not name it a *call*, but I believe that time has proved it was.

My Father was with me at the Firs that summer. And as it happened, he was Mr. Fraser's cabin mate. To my surprise, I found out that Father had invited Mr. Fraser to come and stay with us in Victoria for a week, before he sailed for China in August. That summer we had rented a house at Oak Bay, near the beach, and had room for a visitor.

I was amazed at Father's temerity in inviting Mr. Fraser without consulting Mother, because she and my brother at that time were both opposed to my going as a missionary to China. And Mother was not likely to be pleased at bringing a C.I.M. missionary into her home when she was trying to influence me to be content with Christian work in America! But I was thrilled at the possibility of having a private talk with Mr. Fraser about missionary service. I was hoping to go to Moody Bible Institute that autumn, but the obstacles in my way were so many that I sometimes wondered if they could be from the Lord. I was Mother's only daughter: how important was that? I had made up my mind, during those evening talks on Lisuland, that this unknown missionary was a great man of God. His gifts, apart from his platform ability, were still hidden and unknown to me, but the man himself was obviously walking closely with the Lord. It was one of the thrills of my life in later years, to discover that many far more capable of judging such matters than I, also acclaimed him as one of the great spiritual men of his generation. He is, of course, the hero of the book, *Behind the Ranges*—written many years later after his death by Mrs. Howard Taylor.

Come he did, and by his simple sincerity and kindly interest won the admiration of both my mother and brother. My mother had been a musician before her marriage. She composed music and often wrote the words too, and none of her pieces were ever refused by any publisher to whom she offered them. She just did not go on with it after marriage—that was all. It was in seeking for a contact with Mother that Mr. Fraser suddenly revealed his brilliance at the piano. Mother was enthralled. They "talked music" and Mother knew the names of his teachers and said he had been taught by some of the best masters in London.

But I was watching for a chance to present my own problems, and it came later on in the week. Mr. Fraser wanted to see the beach and I was appointed to take him down one afternoon. We were no sooner alone than I told him I had wanted a talk about my missionary call, so we sat down on the sands by a rocky bit of shore and I told him. I have never forgotten that session.

"Missionary life can be very lonely," he said quietly, and then he proceeded to unfold some of his own early sufferings. I believe now that he did it deliberately to sift me. If I was truly called of God, I would not be discouraged by plain talk of the cost. If I were not called by God, but just had romantic notions of a foreign land, the sooner my gossamer dream was pricked the better. But he little knew the unveiling of his own life that he was unconsciously giving. In fact, as he reminisced he seemed to forget for a while that I was present. His blue-grey eyes brooding out over the sunny, sparkling ocean, he seemed talking to himself. In the quiet of contemplation, as now, they seemed to understand all the sorrows and loneliness that human heart can know. *Acquainted with grief,* they were sad eyes; knowing the victory possible, they were *steadfast and patient.*

I told him of Mother's view and opposition to my call. He answered with the slow drawl which was his when thinking out a question—for none could talk faster than he on occasion. "I have sensed that Satan is opposing you and working through your mother and your brother. We are taught 'whom resist' when it comes to obstacles produced by the devil. I think that should be your stand. In prayer resist the devil, always re-membering to be kind to those who are unconsciously his tools at the moment: II Timothy 2:24. I have a prayer formula which I use on such occasions. It is this: If this obstacle be from Thee, Lord, I accept it: but if it be from Satan, I refuse him and all his works in the name of Calvary. I have found that formula works." I was to use it throughout my life and never found it to fail when prayed with the honest intention of obeying all it implied.

Again he brooded out over the ocean thoughtfully, then added, "I wonder if you will ever get to China. You are very young and you have great obstacles to face. Hm," and again he lapsed into reverie. Then he began to talk as if he knew what to say: "It is even conceivable that *after you get to Moody*, Satan will attempt to get you away. For instance, a telegram might come saying that your mother was very sick and urging you to return home immediately. Now, if that should happen, you cannot leave the moment you get the telegram. You would have to pack your trunk, for instance, and buy a ticket, and so on. Is there any Christian in Vancouver or here whom you can trust to be unprejudiced and yet godly enough to discern such a matter for you?"

"There is Mr. Charles Thomson, Secretary of the C.I.M.," I answered.

"The very man!" he replied quickly. "If you get such a tele-gram, *immediately telegraph to Mr. Thomson*, asking him to check just how ill your mother is. By the time your trunk is packed you should have his reply, and can then see more clearly the path the Lord would have you take."

I listened in awe, but would have been still more amazed if I had known how nearly that prophecy was to be fulfilled.

He that is spiritual judgeth all things (1 Cor. 2:15).

It was an afternoon well spent. Upon the plastic material of a young life had been imprinted standards and ideals which were to last for ever. And a deep glimpse had been afforded me into the life that is hidden in God; the cost of it, the fragrance of it. and the power of it.

CHAPTER EIGHT

THE MOODY BIBLE INSTITUTE

SEPTEMBER 3rd 1924 found me in Chicago, enrolling as a student of the Bible-Missionary course at Moody Bible Institute. This was a most unexpected turn of affairs and not the product of my own planning. I was so very Canadian in loyalty that I would never have chosen to come to the United States for my training. And I admired Professor Ellis so much that I would not have thought of looking beyond the Vancouver Bible School for my missionary preparation. But the Lord took the matter out of my hands.

At the end of the school year 1923-4 I still lacked funds to put me through any Bible school, but outside of my parents and one other I told no one. God, in His wondrous workings, brought that one other person into contact with Miss Marjorie Harrison, whom I had met at the Firs. And it was at the precise moment when she was asking Him how to use some money she had saved that she inadvertently learned that I needed the wherewithal to train for China. *It was Marjorie who chose Moody for me*, directed by the Lord, I am sure. Herself a graduate of the Bible Institute of Los Angeles, and knowing there was this small Bible School right in the city where I was living, she still chose to send me halfway across the continent to Moody. It was the largest Bible institute in the country, and was rich in opportunity for many kinds of Christian work. This latter was what I needed more than I knew. Marjorie explained that her money was limited to that little savings account. She would buy my ticket to Chicago, but could not help me with the return fare! She would pay my board and room for one year, but had no money for my incidental expenses. And she could not help me after that first year. The Moody Bible Institute has an employment bureau which helps students find jobs for odd hours in safe places. For the rest, I must trust the Lord. Was I willing?

Fresh from reading Hudson Taylor's experience in proving God able to supply his need through prayer only, I was thrilled with the opportunity to go on *searching*.

My brother had to make a business trip to Chicago, staying only a few weeks, so I had company across the continent. Dr. Isaac Page met us at the station and took me to M.B.I. Otherwise, I knew no one in that big, whirling metropolis. The Pages had but recently moved to Chicago themselves as deputation workers for the China Inland Mission in the Midwest.

That first day of enrolment, with its trips to this office and that, was bewildering and at the end I was truly weary. I was put into a double room (cheaper) with a strange girl who was European and spoke with a strong accent. The furnishings were very simple, but the house opened right off the street, and, being on the first floor front, people walking along the street passed right under our window. I had never lived in a house which did not have a front enclosure, and it gave me an "exposed" feeling to be so near a public street. This, added to weariness and loneliness, made me homesick. Could I stand it for two years? I was asking myself when a bus rumbled up to a stop at our corner. To sleep with your head just the other side of a wall from such public things seemed almost scandalous. But in another moment I was swung into the heavenlies. The bus was the M.B.I. street meeting group, returning from their first evening's witness and they had begun to sing:

> He makes the path grow brighter
> All along the way:
> He makes the journey lighter
> Every passing day.

Beautiful young voices in four-part harmony sung with a fervent faith in the words that came right from their hearts: it thrilled me through and through. Something in the traffic held them there while they sang it to a finish.

"Oh, Lord," I prayed in ecstasy, "thank You! Thank You! That is to be *the other side* of this 'exposed' existence! Comradeship in the things of Christ and in the cause of soul-winning.

And Christian friends who are my own age and who can sing like that? Oh, thank You, Lord!" I was truly transported into His presence where I nestled down in deep content and fell asleep.

But good things still awaited me. The next day I was called to the phone. It was the Dean's office. "Miss Miller, there is a girl called Lillian Billington, just arrived from Bellingham, who would like to room with you. What is your pleasure in the matter?"

"Oh," I cried, "has she really come? Yes, *please*. I would like so much to be her room-mate. I met her at the Firs Conference. She is a young schoolteacher."

"Yes; that is right," answered the office voice. "But you will have to change your dormitory. We have Miss Billington down for the third floor, Ransom Hall Building, Room 303. Would you kindly proceed to move there as soon as possible, and leave your present room in a proper state for a new occupant? Thank you. Report to us when the move is complete."

Room 303, Ransom Hall, was much larger, higher above the street, so more private, and in every way a happier arrangement to my taste. And best of all, I was to share it with *a girl from the Firs*. We had just met the summer before, but I liked her sweet face. "Billie" and I were happy room-mates for two years. Next door at 304 was a Scottish girl, Anne Barr (who, unknown to us, was to be namesake to my daughter!), and a very unselfish American girl, Ella Dieken, who was later to play a part in my life that the wildest dreams could never have conjured up.

What a meeting Billie and I had! And what fun to help her unpack and find that she had things I didn't—pretty curtains for our windows, cretonne drapes for our trunks, lacy dresser scarfs and so on. Soon our room was transformed into a real girls' bower, and my beauty-loving soul was deeply grateful.

Mealtime was an adventure. Hundreds of students all eating at once. Oh the noise of the talk, the clatter of the cutlery or dishes. The men sat on one side and the women on the other, twelve to a table. A senior and a junior student sat one at each end, but the rest of us changed seats each day. When you arrived at a certain seat you automatically became waitress for the table for that day. One waitress removed the dirty dishes; another had the duty of going early into the kitchen and bringing in the hot food, and must go for "seconds" when necessary.

I was waiting in line one day for the hot vegetables; as soon as the bell went they would be dished out to us, but there was still a moment before the hour struck. I was dreaming of Lisuland, when turning around suddenly I encountered the eyes of another dreamer—the young man who ran the dish-washing machine. It was one of those shock-encounters when you find yourself already over the threshold and into the other fellow's soul before there is time to knock for admission. Very embarrassing. Each of us looked away quickly and pretended not to notice, but it had happened. From then on I was conscious of that dish-washer! Whether he was full-time kitchen employee or student-help I did not know. The annoying thing was that I had become conscious of him. Now, I had made up my mind that I was not going to have any boy-friends at Moody. I had proved that they were distracting and I wanted these two years to be given to unhindered preparation for my life work in China. So I was extremely cross with myself to find that as soon as I entered the kitchen I looked to see if he was there or not. To discipline myself, I did not inquire his name or his status; but frequently I had to carry dishes past him and I felt sure he knew my name and all about me. And I was correct: he did. But he never tried to speak: I did appreciate that. I did not know that he had come to Moody vowing to have nothing to do with girls—lest they distract him from his studies. But he had made inquiries as to who the girl was who wore the green blouse trimmed with brown swan's down.

Shortly after my arrival, Dr. and Mrs. Page had invited me to supper in their apartment. He had long been my father's close friend and I had called him Daddy Page for years. After I had taken off my wraps, he thrust a bundle of photographs of Moody and Moody students into my hands, excusing himself while he went to help his wife in the kitchen. As I looked over them I came across one which greatly attracted me. It was a girl's face, and there was character as well as beauty there.

"Oh, Daddy Page," I cried. "Who is this? What a lovely face! Is she here at the Institute?"

He came in and looked over my shoulder. "Oh that," he said. "Yes, Isobel. She *is* a lovely girl. Her name is Kathryn Kuhn, but she has just graduated and gone on to Wheaton. I wish you could meet her. She has a brother here at the Institute."

"Oh yes?" I said politely and quickly changed the conversation. But inwardly I said, "Well, if her brother looks like she does, I'll stay away from him. Here's where you don't go to any mixed parties, Isobel Miller!"

And, apart from the Freshman Reception, I quietly refused invitations to any party or picnic where the other sex would be present—that is, during my first term. It was my second term before I found it had all been in vain.

It was months before I learned that the dishwasher in the kitchen was the brother of Kathryn Kuhn!

Of my studies during those two years and four months (I was ill and lost a term) I can only glance at the blessing they brought me. Dr. James Gray was President then and I was privileged to have a class under him. Bible analysis under Dr. Jaderquist was an outstanding joy, and I later passed it on to the Lisu church, analysing First and Second Peter with our Bible School students. Those notes are still being used.

Dr. Elbert McCreery taught me comparative religions and phonetics and was one of my favourite teachers. He was himself the blessing, with his gentle, Christ-like life.

Dr. Robert Glover made me sit on the edge of my seat, week after week, as he presented the challenge of missions, and in another class taught the history of missions. His fire continually enkindled my own.

Talmadge Bittikofer taught us part-singing and conducting, which I was to use constantly with the Lisu church. We all loved "Bitti" and his solos stirred me to the depths. He sang his message right into your heart.

So one could go on, but I think the greatest thing Moody did for me was in the practical work assignments. Mrs. F. C. Allison

was in charge of these. Every student had to take one or more
such assignments each week; and your assignments were changed
each term, so that you got a great variety. Open-air meetings
among the Jews would likely mean rotten eggs and tomatoes
pelted at you, so you wore your oldest clothes (I was knocked off
the pavement into the street once when my turn came for Jewish
work). Sunday school classes and hospital or jail visitation were
considered easiest and my kindly Lord started me off gently.
A slip of paper from the Practical Work Department told
me I was assigned to teach a Sunday school class and do
visitation during the week in the Italian slums. I would work
under senior student Miss Ethel Thompson, Room X, 830
Building, and would I please report to her immediately for
instructions.

So behold a young Moody freshman climbing the stairs of the
830 Building and standing before a closed bedroom door about
to knock. What would Miss Thompson be like? How could I
ever do slum visitation? How my heart beat as I firmly knocked
at that door. Once it opened, I was *in for it*; that is, I must plunge
into soul-winning from which my shyness had always shrunk.

It was opened by a short, slim young woman, perhaps in her
early thirties, who, when she heard my name, welcomed me
quickly with a soft, southern drawl in her voice. After asking me
to sit down, she began: "I suppose I had better tell you about our
assignment. We are working under a Community House or
Church in the Italian quarter. On Sundays we are in charge of the
Primary Department and we have full liberty to preach the
gospel there. They think we cannot hurt the little ones! Because,
you see, the minister in charge is a modernist and he conducts
dances on Sunday evening and so on. This is our big difficulty
and the most discouraging featuer.

"During the week we go into the homes—tenement houses,
knock at doors and present our message. The people are poor,
of course, and many of them Roman Catholics. But there have
been a few decisions for Christ.

"Personally, I think the work needs prayer almost more than
anything else," and she eyed this new freshman questioningly,
wondering what the Lord had sent her in me.

E

Remembering Mr. Fraser's lessons on the place of prayer in Christian service, I answered eagerly: "Oh, I believe in prayer too! I'd be happy to come over here to your room every day for a time of prayer together?"

"Would you?" said "Tommy" (none of the students called her *Ethel*. She was *Tommy* Thompson to us all) and her face lit up with hope and joy. "All right. I'm working my way through school here and so I am busy, but half an hour before noon each day—how would that suit you?" It fit in my schedule and became an important part of my life.

That first Sunday Tommy took me to the community centre and introduced me to the Rev. K——, the minister-in-charge, as her new helper. "Fine," he said. "How about having lunch with us today? I told the wife there would be a new worker and we ought to get acquainted—she's prepared."

That meant we stayed for the morning service and heard the usual liberal kind of sermon from Mr. K——; something on courage or high ideals or one of such verbal essays; but nothing in it to bring new life to anyone.

At dinner afterwards, in their apartment, he said to us rather patronizingly, "You know, girls, I used to believe like you do. In fact, you may be surprised to learn that I am a Moody graduate myself. But after graduation I went into a seminary and there learned that no one nowadays believes in that old-fashioned stuff. I lost my faith, as you call it, at seminary. But somehow our liberalism does not energize people like the Moody teaching seems to, and so when I found out how dead the work here is, I asked for a couple of Moody students to be sent us (you work without salary!)"—this with a grin—"to stir up interest in the neighbourhood. You bring them in and we'll mould them into a good community!"

We ignored the comment that rose so quickly to our lips, and I said, "This is very strange, Mr. K——. You have departed from the old faith and I have just departed from liberalism to return to the faith! I lost my belief in God in college, but I have done some personal investigation in the matter and I'm convinced that He is, and the only way to Him is through faith in the atoning power of the blood of Christ to bring forgiveness of sins and eternal life. You and I are a contrasting pair—you have entered The Misty Flats whilst I have just found my way out of them back on to the High Way again."

He was truly moved. His eyes sparkled and he leaned forward, plying me with questions; he was sarcastic, argumentative, but deeply interested. Tommy sat quiet, praying. She had never heard my story, but recognized instantly the working of the Spirit of God.

When it came time to leave, Mr. K—— was belligerent again. "You're too intelligent a girl to slip back into that old stuff," he challenged me. "We'll have to have some more talks about this! You girls will have to come to supper some night after your visitation work." And so we left.

On the long car ride home Tommy said, "I believe God has already begun to answer our prayers. Just think of His sending a worker who had been through all this liberal stuff that is binding this man from any power really to help change lives! I watched his face while you talked and many of your points went home, though he was too proud to acknowledge it. I've got faith now to believe that God will bring Mr. K—— back to the faith! Let us agree together on Matthew 18:19 and add this request to our daily prayers. Now, let's see—we go visiting in the homes on Thursday, is it?" I myself forget which day of the week we were assigned for visitation, but I can never forget those experiences.

Tommy proved to be a most rare companion. She had a keen sense of humour, and droll wit simply poured from her. Visitation was in itself a grim experience for me. Those dark, dirty tenement houses, with broken stairs, bad plumbing which often made the place reek, whole families cooped up in one small room sometimes, would have terrified me. But Tommy always had a merry retort or comment for a stumbled toe or an offended nose; a remark so pungent in its truth and applicability that I was shaken with laughter as well as with distaste. Then it was always she who took the brunt of the first attack, so to speak. She was an artist at a tactful approach, and I sat at her feet and tried to learn. Over thirty years have passed since those days, so I cannot remember conversations or her delightful wit

But I remember one incident. In a long, dark hall of an old tenement house we went from door to door, seeking entrance and conversation. One was opened by a big brute of a man who scowled at us and shouted, "What are you after? What ya doin' here?"

"Brother," smiled up Tommy at him with her soft, southern drawl, "we're a couple of friends who are interested in seeing that you get a better deal. Won't you let us come in and talk a moment?"

"Ah, come on," growled the man suspiciously. "Nobody's really interested in helping us. What's your line? Salesman? Politics? Whatever it is, we ain't interested," and he moved the door as if to bang it in our faces.

"Now, brother," piped up Tommy plaintively, "a pair of poor tired girls can't hurt a big fellow like you. Won't you even offer us a chair a moment? We've been on our feet for hours and we did hope——" A woman's voice from within: "They can sit down a moment, Bill. I know what it is to have tired feet."

Bill cursed bitterly, but left the door open, turned and stalked to the far side of the dismal room. Then Tommy, with a droll remark about her feet, made the woman laugh and a conversation was soon under way. However, the Lord's name was no sooner uttered than Bill appeared in our midst again, eyes blazing with anger.

"So it's religious sluts you are! That's the worst of all! I'm not going to have any blankety blank"—he swore profusely—"whinings around here! I'm an atheist, I am"—and so on.

Tommy turned on her loving, merry humour. I do not know how she did it, except the Spirit of God was working with her, but she had him quietened and listening before we left. I think, too, his wife decided for Christ. Almost every visitation day, some soul made that decision. Dear Tommy, it was she who taught me that "loving folks" is the only way to approach them for the Lord Jesus.

In the Primary Department God began to work too. The children started to ask the Lord to come into their hearts. Mr. K—— was interested and indifferent by turns. Sometimes he would ignore us for weeks, almost as if antagonistic; then again he would come into our Sunday school, listen and watch; and invite us around for a meal.

How we laboured in prayer for him. Tommy with her cute remarks in the dark hallways of tenement houses was one person; on her knees praying for the salvation of souls and the reclamation of Mr. K—— was quite a different person; yet the two sides of her character blended into one another. If you only heard her jokes, you would never have guessed at her tears and her passionate pleadings for sin-bound souls.

In my second term I asked to be reappointed to the same assignment as both Tommy and I felt the Lord's work was not completed yet in that place. But that was the term when I fell ill and lost six weeks of study and of course could not go with Tommy. At the end of that term she graduated and left for Mexico. But there is one precious thing yet to record.

After I was out of the infirmary and just before Tommy left the Institute, we were both called down to the Reception Room one day. To our surprise, it was Mr. K——. He was a changed man; his very face had that gentle, chastened look upon it, but there was also a light there we had never seen before.

"I just called you girls to tell you that the Lord has answered your prayers for me. I have come back to Himself. It has been a bitter fight, as you doubtless have watched and seen. Pride refused to be crucified for a long time. But it was weekly more evident to me that the Word you girls preached was the power of God unto salvation. Lives were changed through your ministry—my honesty had to admit it. Nobody was changed through mine. Maybe you don't know that I began to preach the Bible again as I saw how God used your Bible teaching. But nothing happened. Then I had to come to the place where I was willing to preach the Cross of Christ as the only way; the blood of the Redeemer as the only atonement for our sins. *That worked*—for me as well as for you. There has been an awful fuss. I made a confession in the pulpit and stopped the Sunday dances. My church filled for service, but the Committee got wind of it and were very angry." Tears came to his eyes. "They dismissed me, in short; but I have got a little country church appointment now and I'll be moving the family out there. And I can preach the truth there. My wife is whole-heartedly with me and we both feel we have to thank you two. God bless you. And *God bless the school that D. L. Moody founded.*"

Heartily, with tears in our eyes and awe in our hearts we said, "Amen." We never saw him again.

CHAPTER NINE

SPIRITUAL PREVISION

IT was in December 1924, that I received a letter from my mother saying that she was facing the possibility of an operation. It was discovered that she had a tumour and there was a choice before her; radiology treatments over quite a long period or surgery. She was inclined to have the latter as being less drawn-out; "get it over" instead of many long trips to town, which the radiology would necessitate. But I had not heard definitely what her decision had been when a telegram arrived saying she was with the Lord. She had chosen surgery and had died in the hospital. Father wired me lovingly, but said the funeral would be over before I could reach home, so I should not try to come.

This was a shattering blow to me. My mother had opposed my going to the foreign field because of her clinging love for me, her only daughter. In the agony of her pleadings with me she had said some bitter things which at the time I had not taken to heart, as I recognized they were the upflinging of violent emotion and not the result of considered thought. But one word had been: "You are praying to go to China and God answers prayer; but you will only go over my dead body." Of course, that word now came back to me and simply lacerated my heart.

I owe a great deal to my mother. She had deep affections, high ideals and was very conscientious. She sacrificed her musical career and many opportunities for a musical evening with other young people in order to baby-sit with her two children at home. She was married young and was still in her twenties when my brother and I were born: she had great ambitions for us and carefully watched over us. We were never allowed to "run the streets." She gave up her evenings to reading to us and planning to make home a pleasant place where our friends were welcome. She was a Christian, at one time a consecrated Christian, and always trained us to love the Lord and honour His Word. As we grew older she wanted us "to move in good society," and this was the temptation which had led her to compromise with worldly things. But at the root of it was her love for us.

I had never known life without my mother. I took her affection for granted as I accepted the warmth of the daily sunshine, and in such careless security I had not shown her the gratitude which was her due. All these things came to me, now that she was gone: it was too late to express my thanks to her, and my heart was sorely torn.

During that Christmas vacation I took employment as a waitress in a restaurant.

School reopened in January. I do not remember the date, but one day in class a messenger went up to the platform and interrupted the teacher. He read it and said: "Will Miss Isobel Miller please go to the office of the Dean of Women? There is a telegram for you."

Perfectly astounded and wondering, I got up and sped toward the Women's Building. What could it be? I was trembling by the time I reached the office and from the Dean's face I knew it was bad news of some kind. I could only look at her in agony and beg that she tell me quickly and not prolong suspense. She did so. "Sit down, dear. The telegram reads: FATHER FATALLY INJURED IN ELEVATOR ACCIDENT. COME HOME AT ONCE. MURRAY. Who is Murray?"

"My brother," I choked. "Oh, but I can't stand it. Father too! Oh."

"Is there anyone we can call to help you, dear?" she asked tenderly.

Suddenly I was far away, sitting on a seaside beach beside a tall, strong man who was looking out over the breaking sea with brooding eyes, and he was saying, "Satan may try to get you away from the Institute. Is there anyone you know who can be depended on for Godly, unprejudiced judgment?" In a flash I recognized that Mr. Fraser's foresight had come true: he had just missed the instrument used, that was all. He had thought it would be Mother, and it turned out to be my brother who summoned me home. It steadied and quieted me.

Sitting up, I said, "Yes, please. I would like Dr. Isaac Page to come and help me."

The Dean was relieved to be able to do something, and in a moment she was talking to him on the phone. I heard him say, "I'll take a taxi and be there immediately." I waited in the Dean's office until he arrived—my father's intimate friend.

"Daddy Page," I said, "Mr. Fraser told me this might happen. *He also told me what to do if it did happen.* I will go and pack my trunk, but will you please do two things for me? Reserve a ticket for the train tonight, but don't buy it yet. Wire immediately to Mr. Charles Thomson and ask if Dad is as bad as Murray said?"

"Excellent idea, Isobel," said Dr. Page. "First reports of these accidents are often excited and exaggerated. Mr. Thomson will know. I will go and do that immediately—there is no train going to Vancouver until this evening, anyway. And you? You will *trust and not be afraid*?"

"Yes," I said, much calmer now that a plan of activity was under way. "Thank you. Everyone here is so kind and loving to me. I will be all right."

"I'll come back just as soon as I have wired and made the train reservation," he said, and was gone.

Before supper that evening the answering telegram arrived. It read: FATHER IMPROVING SENDS LOVE AND SAYS STAY AT YOUR POST WRITING THOMSON.

Oh what a relief. The letter that followed told how the elevator girl had lost control and the cage had crashed four storeys on to a cement basement. Daddy was injured inwardly, and the jar began a trouble which did finally take his life, but he lived for nearly twenty happy years before that took place!

"He that is spiritual judgeth all things" (1 Cor. 2:15).

How did Mr. Fraser know? When God's child is living close to Him and perfectly yielded to His will (some phrase it *being filled with the Spirit*) it is possible for such an one to spread his mind out in the Lord's presence and catch the instruction of God especially if interceding for someone else. If there was no God this could not be. Satan can read man's thought and describe the past, he can use intelligence and *guess* at the future, but he cannot *know* the future.

This experience was followed closely by another special instance of the Spirit's operation.

The Otis Whipple family were, at this time, no longer in Seattle, but in China. Mr. Whipple is a fine architect and he had been called to build a mission hospital in one of the big inland cities. He took his family with him, so it was some little time before Mrs. Whipple heard of my sorrows.

One day I got a letter from her. It said something like this: "Isobel, I feel your mother was spiritually prepared to go home. It was very strange. I knew nothing of the possibility of her operation, let alone her danger, but the day of her death I was so burdened for her I spent a long time in prayer for her and had an assurance that she was at last yielded to God's will in all things.

"But now as I write I have another burden that presses upon me. It is for you, and *somehow connected with your father*. I am in much prayer for you, dear, and for him. I do not know what is happening, but God has called me today to intercede for you both and claim only His will to be done upon each of you."

I looked up the date. It was the very day of the telegram of father's accident! Mrs. Whipple was in inland China, halfway around the world; she had no human knowledge whatever of that which had taken place. She could not possibly know (for I did not know myself for several months) that before she went to the hospital mother admitted that I had chosen the better course in pursuing the will of God. What had been worldly ambition in her life she confessed to Him and came back to her earlier consecration of all to her Lord, before she died. And who knows how much Mrs. Whipple's intercession helped to win that battle?

Of course, I was deeply impressed. Wistfully I wondered if I would ever attain to the place where God could trust me with His counsels in this way. I did not know that God has these gifts in greater or less measure for all who are born again in the Spirit and living in obedience to that Holy Spirit. I was soon to learn.

Joy at Father's recovery was quickly followed by a new anxiety. Mother had been the business head in the family and it was she who had managed to make ends meet, and who had planned so carefully that I was able to get an education. Father was of Micawber's optimistic and gullible temperament. He was always going to "strike it rich" by investment in copper mines, silver mines, gold mines, etc. The fact that he had consistently lost all his life savings in these "promising" stocks never seemed to teach him. After Mother's death I was perturbed to hear that father had given up his profession and gone in for stock-selling—a new invention which would make us all millionaires in a short time! Brother, too, had sold his chicken ranch, and apparently was not working at anything. Why start something new if you are going to be independently wealthy soon? They had rented a little bungalow in North Vancouver, sold some of our furniture and moved the rest in. These cheerful, wonderful-sounding letters only served to burden me: the higher Dad's expectations rose, the lower sank my heart!

"Lord, is life to be always grim?" I whispered to Him. His answer was not long in coming.

It was in the General Missions class that Dr. Glover repeated a previous announcement. "I have told you before," he said, "of the Foreign Missions Convention of the United States and Canada to be held in Washington, D.C., January 28 to February 2. The Moody Bible Institute has been allotted eight delegates, but we only have six signed up to go. This will be a wonderful experience, since famous missionaries and native converts from all over the world are coming. President Coolidge is to open the session. I am sure there are some in the student body who can afford to pay their own way. The time is getting short. I would urge you to sign up. Next week is the last opportunity, so get ready."

Delegate to the great missionary conference in the capital city! My heart reached out in longing to go. Suddenly I felt I was to go. It was as if the Lord said, "You've had a long enough siege of sorrow, dear. I'm going to send you to Washington for a little time of joy." I thrilled through and through and believed Him. Yet it was an impossible hope; I had not a cent I could put towards it. All week long I imagined the Lord sending me a huge gift of money and my trotting up to Dr. Glover and offering to be a delegate; but not a cent came in.

The last day of opportunity arrived. At missions class that morning several student volunteers had been asked to speak three minutes each, telling why they felt they should go to the foreign field, and at the end Dr. Glover again made an impassioned plea for one more delegate to the Washington Conference. The opportunity closed that night, he said. I left the class wondering: Had it been the voice of the Lord? Had I been deceived by wishful thinking? That noon there was a note in my mail box. *Call at Dr. Glover's office immediately*, it read. With high-bounding heart I simply ran to the building where the Director of Missions had his office and, trembling with excitement, I knocked at the door.

"Come in! Oh Miss Miller, sit down." And Dr. Glover beamed at me. "I sent for you to tell you that someone has offered to pay your way to the Washington Conference. Would you like to go?"

"Oh," I gasped. "*Would I?* But who could it be?" (Dr. and Mrs. Page? But how could they afford it. Oh, who could it be?)

"The donor wishes to remain unknown. I believe she is a stranger to you," he smiled. "She." Then it was a woman? "She has paid your fare, your hotel fees and meals and given an extra twenty for just fun. Here it is. The fare and hotel bill I'll pay for you. Now, you'll have to be ready to leave by tomorrow. Can you make it? I have already got permission for you from the Dean of Women."

It is needless to say I was able to make it!

But I would like to tell you how God worked this out for me, for the dear benefactress did allow me to know the story later on. She was a well-to-do Christian recently widowed. That Thursday morning she happened to be downtown on business near the Institute, and, glancing at her watch, she saw there was time to slip in and listen to Dr. Glover's mission hour. As she slipped into a seat among the students, I was called upon to give my testimony. When I was through Mrs. X whispered to the girl seated next to her, "Who was that speaker?" We neither of us knew who that girl was, but she not only told my name; she added, "She has been going through deep sorrow. Her mother died before Christmas and a few weeks later her father was nearly killed in an accident." The kind little widow's heart went out to me, her own bereavement still fresh upon her; so when Dr. Glover arose to make a last plea for the one remaining delegate, she felt instantly that she would like to send me. "A change of scene, inspiring messages, sightseeing around the capitol," she thought. "Just what that girl needs. I'll give it to her, and incidentally M.B.I. can have its full quota of delegates." God bless His generous stewards who live in the flow of His thoughts, so that He can think and act through them.

Such spiritual premonitions I never had before I found the Lord. From time to time I have had them ever since. I believe they are given for the purpose of comfort and to refresh our experience *that He is there*, and that He cares. Only God could have worked out that little forecast and fulfilment.

And so began one of the high peaks of joy which tower up exultantly above the painful valley experiences of my life. It was one that has always been outstanding; and it moulded my life as I little suspected it would have any power to do, for one of the other eight delegates was John B. Kuhn.

I had been formally introduced to him at last, and it was at a mixed party after all! The occasion was Daddy Page's birthday, when a group of the young student volunteers whom the Pages had often had at their home decided to give him a surprise party! I was told there would be boys present and also told that one of these would be that brother of Kathryn Kuhn, so I knew I was to meet him at last. But how could I get out of it? If it had been any staff member's birthday I could have found an excuse. But my own dear Daddy Page—I just *had* to go to his birthday party!

The group were to meet at Clark Street corner, where we caught the 7.30 p.m. street-car. We girls arrived first, and the moon was rising over the tall old houses when we saw the boys' group approaching. "Oh, here they come!" cried the leader of us girls. "Miss Miller, let me introduce Jack Graham and John

Kuhn and . . ." I heard no more. I found myself looking straight into the face of—the dishwasher from the Bible Institute kitchen!

I might add that it was a wonderful convention with world-renowned missionaries taking part. We heard them speak and met some of them personally. In between meetings we went sight-seeing. We visited the White House and were presented to President Coolidge, shaking hands with him. And after it was over we all had a short trip to Mount Vernon to see the home of George and Martha Washington. Sitting together; eating together; sight-seeing through snow-slushy Washington; laughter and teasing when we set out to buy Gordon Hedderly Smith some galoshes, only to hear one store say they did not carry such a large size!

How little we knew of the future years. That two of the delegates would marry each other and serve Him in far off Lisuland; that Jack Graham would be in the same province, ministering to the Miao tribe; that Irene Forsythe would have a wonderful ministry in Shantung Province among the Chinese; that Gordon Smith would open up work among many new tribes in Indo-China. Friendships were formed during those delegate days that have sweetened the whole road of life ever since.

CHAPTER TEN

AT SUNDRY TIMES AND IN DIVERS MANNERS

WHEN is the Search ended? In one sense, it is finished when our hand, stretched out to God in the name of His appointed mediator Jesus Christ, feels the answering grasp and knows that He is there. But in another sense the searching never ends, for the first discovery is quickly followed by another, and that by another, and so it goes on. As I write it is dawning a new day. The far horizon has seen the bright spot of the rising sun, but heavy clouds soon covered it. However, these clouds have become illuminated and streaks of pink and gold beauty are breaking through chance rents in their filmy cover. One discovers glory after glory as the eye eagerly explores the heavens. And so it is with God. To find *that He is*, is the mere starting-point of our search. We are lured on to explore *what He is*, and that search is never finished, and it grows more thrilling the farther one proceeds.

Up to this point I have discovered that God is; and that He is mine by the mediatorship of Christ. I have discovered that He can and will teach me His way, or His plan for my life. I have found that He can overcome obstacles and that we do not need to arouse a great hullabaloo to get Him to do so. Hudson Taylor was right in his discovery: "learn to move man, through God, by prayer alone." By searching I have discovered that He has strange and sweet ways of manifesting Himself; at sundry times and in divers manners God is still speaking (Heb. 1:1).

This chapter will deal with the simple dry fact of finances. Elsewhere I have told how He provided, through Marjorie Harrison, for my fare to Chicago, board and room there for one year. I also told of a second provision most unexpectedly made to care for extras, such as winter clothing which was needed for the more severe climate of the mid-west. I will not repeat those stories, but will go on to His provision for the autumn term of 1925, when Marjorie's money had all been used up and I was entirely dependent on my own earnings and God's care for the rest. But this involves the story of another life which had touched mine the previous spring.

It must have been about April 1925, that I was struck by a prayer request given in the evening devotions hour. A graduate student got up and asked prayer for "a girl-friend who has had a terrible tragedy happen to her, and she has lost her faith. She is coming to see me on a visit here to the Institute. Pray she may find the Lord again."

A girl, struck by heartbreak, pushed on to The Misty Flats and was floundering bitterly—I saw it all with a sympathy that pierced my heart. "Lord, *give her to me*" I prayed inwardly. "Oh I can understand how she feels!" I felt He answered that He would. Humanly speaking, there was no likelihood of our meeting in the ordinary course of events. I was now working part-time as a noon rush-hour waitress, and the graduate student who had given out the request moved in a different circle from me. "The élite" we laughingly dubbed those students who were wealthy enough to go through Moody without working their way. They had plenty of leisure time and we had none; so "the élite" and "the workers" seldom met outside of classrooms. They had picnics and parties for which we could not afford the time and naturally each group clanned together. I could have pushed my way up to the graduate student and asked for an introduction; I would have been nicely received. But I decided if it were of the Lord, He must work it out His way, then I would know that it was not just my own impulsive wishing. But I prayed about it.

Now the strange thing is that neither Ruth nor I can remember how it came about! I have a dim recollection of a chance encounter in the post office. I, of course, was watching the élite set for the appearance of a stranger and so spotted her early. She was tall, slim, with light brown hair naturally curly, and the soft accent of a Southerner. But why she noticed me among the hundreds of unfamiliar girl-faces at M.B.I., I will never know. God answered my prayer and "gave" me Ruth—that is all I need to say.

Soon she was coming to our room for talks and pursuing me wherever she could catch this student labourer. I remember once encountering her just before the noon hour, when I was rushing off to be waitress at that restaurant (the employees' restaurant of a huge corporation nearby).

"I want to talk to you!" she said.

"Fine," I answered. "Can you come in tonight? I'm on my way to my job now and dare not stop—I'll just barely make it."

"No!" petulantly. "I want to talk *now*. I'll walk with you to your job—nothing against that, is there, ma'am?" (We had great fun over the difference in Canadian and Southern speech-forms. To me *ma'am* was the language of a servant to a mistress; to her it was the polite way to apologize. She laughed much, and mimicked drolly my "I beg your pardon?" and rubbed in her *ma'am* as often as possible with a teasing sparkle in her eyes.)

Now, I was just a little diffident about Ruth seeing me in that restaurant. I was servant to the servants there, so to speak, and the rush-hour girls had to take left-over apron uniforms, usually very ill-fitting ones. Ruth was the only child of well-to-do people, and cultured homes were native diet. What would she say if she saw me in that restaurant? But she was quick to notice my slight hesitation in accepting her escort, and nothing would shake her off from that moment. Right into the restaurant she came and saw it all; saw, too, my embarrassment, and mischievously determined to make the most of it.

Ruth was the twentieth-century counterpart of Mary Tudor—sister of Henry VIII. Charming, capricious, affectionate and utterly lovable, clever and nimble-witted, she was still untamed; or to use a more vulgar but more explicit word—*unspanked*. Her parents had spared the rod, and that always follows a child through the rest of life.

It was impossible ever to "handle" Ruth. She saw you tuck the handle under your apron just as soon as you moved your arm, and with an almost devilish mischief she would whisk it out and brandish it before your chagrined face and defy you. She was my superior in personality, brains, social culture—in everything but one thing. She did not possess the fellowship of the Lord Jesus or know Him as I did—and that was what I longed that she

F

might. But I had not been with her long before I knew that I could never "deal" with her. She was too quick to recognize any such effort, and she had my own resentment at the invasion of her spiritual sanctum. She would open it up when and where she liked, but no one should knock it open. The only thing I knew to do was—to love her and pray for her.

Somewhere along the line (maybe an evening session, relaxed on her bed, talking in the dark) she suddenly opened up and told me her tragedy. She had become engaged to one of God's finest gentlemen; one who knew Him and served Him devoutly. But they had had a quarrel and Ruth had high-handedly broken their engagement. She had had an unfortunate experience with a religious hypocrite, and with her lightning-like petulance had said that she could not believe in God when a Christian would act like that. She had never meant to really break with Jack, she loved him too dearly for that. But she had conceived a pique against life for disappointing her and had to take it out on someone. The first overture Jack made, she would melt and be his own darling Ruth again—that was her inward thought. But no overture came. She did not know that even whilst she "tiff-ed" with him, he was going down with a fever. When she did learn it, he was already in Heaven.

Yes, it is better to have the rod when you are a child. When life must wield it against you, it is too cruel. Can you think what her agonies were? Not just to have lost him (their wedding date had been set) but to have him go before she was able to say, "Oh, I did not mean it! I'm sorry. Please forgive."

Her kind, worldly father did the best he knew. He handed her his cheque-book and said, "Go to New York and have a good time. Forget the irrevocable." She went. And all the wild life she led I did not care to hear. Just one question was making my heart stand still: "Ruth, you did not *grope for the low road?*"

She was silent a moment. "I know what you mean. No. Somehow there has always been in me a hidden passion for chastity. But just everything else I did—I was wild."

I sighed a "Thank God!" "He had wallowed in fleshly things until his appetites had become fibrous"—that is what the low road does. Christ *can* save from it, as praise God our city rescue missions all testify, but it leaves scars. As for the hidden passion for chastity, I understood that too.

> Hast thou heard Him, seen Him, known Him?
> Is not thine a captured heart?

Anyone who has ever really known the Lord, even only in reflection, can never again be satisfied with less.

"Did the cheque-book and New York's wildest—*help*?" I asked.

She withered me with a look. "You know it didn't."

How I prayed for this dear honest, if wilful, young life. I thought I had been able to help her out from The Misty Flats, but later she was sucked back in again. However, she is His now. In my Moody Autograph book (which is a large tome!) her autograph covers four pages, written in three instalments. The first is one of her nonsense poems, shrewd with perspicuity. (She has a literary gift, among other things. The élite publishing houses reach after her manuscripts! They do not even know that I exist.) But the third reads as follows:

Third Instalment.
Wonder if I'll ever finish this! Sounds like The Perils of Ruth in three instalments. What I've been trying to say for the last two pages is that I love you (just plain, unadulterated, simple-minded love). You have meant so very much to me—you, yourself—and you have meant infinitely more in that you have both *showed* me the way and *fought with* me during these hard hard days of decision. I can wish no greater thing than that you may mean just that to these dear folks in China.

I know that Ruth had been "sifting" me. When she caught a glimpse of pride wincing, she seized on it and walked right to the restaurant to see every bit of it. More than that, at a later date, without any warning, she brought a college girl-friend with her to that same restaurant to catch me as I was; which they did!

But she did more than just sift. Tenderly affectionate and generous, she discovered that I enjoyed beautiful things. Maybe it began by her getting permission from the Dean to take me out for a meal—so we would have that much more time to talk.

My frank delight in the harmonious drapes, shaded lights, soft
classical dinner music amused Ruth. From then on she deliberately hunted up quaint, pretty tea-rooms and increased her
invitations! With her unfailing charm, she could wangle a
permission out of a Dean that no one else would even dare to
propose! And so she "embroidered" my days.

But her careless use of money shocked me. When away from
Chicago she once sent me a telegram, in lieu of a letter! When
I remonstrated (by two-cent post) I received a second telegram to
laugh at me! No, you could not "handle" Ruth!

But there came a day when, to her astonishment, she found
that someone else could be hard to handle too. The summer of
1925 I spent in Canada with my Aunt Nellie, mother's younger
sister. On returning to the Institute I now faced having to support
myself entirely, as said above. This meant working three times
a day instead of only at noon, but I was highly favoured. I had
obtained the post of waitress at the faculty table in the Institute
dining-room. This meant being down a half-hour before each
meal in order to prepare the food nicely, and it meant staying
half an hour afterward to wash up and to set the table, and then
there was the time consumed in having my meal when other
students were already through. But it was not too strenuous;
it was among Christians (no more heathen Americans shouting
at me!); it was exacting, for you had to be there right on time,
but it was at no great distance away, such as the other job had
been. No time wasted in getting there.

One day I was in the act of preparing a meal when in breezed
Ruth! She had arrived unexpectedly with her parents for a short
visit. "So this is what we are now!" she teased. "Say, I've got
something to tell you." With an eye on the clock hand which
was travelling close toward my deadline, I said, "Keep it, dearie,
until tonight—can you? I'm dying to hear it, but my job has to
come first. I've got to get this finished before the faculty arrive.
I'm working full-time this term" (there would be no more meals
out in pretty tea-rooms).

Ruth stood and pouted. "But I want to talk to you about my
soul!" (Twinkle in her eye) "How important is *that*? And you
stand there flaying radishes into rose-buds and say, 'Another

time.' How do you know I'll feel like talking about it at another time? There is something wrong here. Something's got to be done about this," and then she had to leave as the faculty were beginning to arrive.

I felt very uncomfortable. 'Twas so. Ruth wasn't the kind that could open up the doors of her sanctum just at any odd moment. But then—I had to work, and surely the Lord expected faithfulness in my job? Inwardly I prayed for help and went on with the task in hand.

But Ruth was busy too. She arrived in my room that evening her old gay self. "I've got it all arranged!" she said happily. "No more table-serving for Little Pats!" That was her pet name for me. (Apparently I am addicted to short, quick movements when showing affection—many short, little kisses, and many little pats on the back in a hug. My children laugh at the former and Ruth declared she got homesick for the latter—the name has pursued me through the years.)

"I told my father about you, and he says he will be delighted to support you through the rest of your schooling here. Now then! Whenever Ruthie arrives and needs talking to, she can have it. And many others too. Don't you see the Lord's hand in this—*ma'am*?"—with roguish delight.

But I didn't, and there was an awkward silence. Ruth's father was a fine, clean man, *but he played the races*, and gained his money in the usual worldly ways. Hudson Taylor believed firmly that God does not need, and will not use for blessing, the money offered by unbelievers. He is able to provide for His own children apart from help from those who serve Mammon. "We can afford to have as little as the Lord chooses to give, but we cannot afford to have *unconsecrated money*," he once said. But would Ruth ever be able to understand what I meant by refusing on that score? Her eyes sparkled with mischievous delight when I said her father's money was *unconsecrated*—she would have a good time telling him that! Miserably, I tried to explain without appearing ungrateful. But when she saw that it really touched what was sacred to me, she accepted quietly, for Ruth was a lady born. When her visit ended I was still faculty waitress.

But I had not counted on Ruth's decisiveness. After a week or so, I received a letter from her; I wish I had it to quote now, for nothing reveals her charm as much as her little notes. It simply stated that she had got herself a job—teaching physical culture at their local Y.W.C.A., and her monthly salary was enough to pay my room and board. Now, was that consecrated enough for me to use—*ma'am*? Not a cent of her father's should taint it! "Now, Lambkins, you know it will be good for Ruth to have to hold down a job! Now don't you? Just think of the good you are doing me by accepting and thus making me an honest worker in the hive of life, and not a drone? *Please* write and tell me you accept?"

And so you see, she had "handled" me after all. I never was able to handle her! But that is how the Lord sent me support for the term September-December 1925.

Christmas 1925, I was invited to the Harrison home for the holidays. Dr. and Mrs. Norman B. Harrison were now living in St. Louis, where he was pastor of the famous old Washington-Compton Presbyterian Church. They have a family of six talented children, and with two or three of us guests added we made an hilarious house-party. Members of his congregation invited us out to meals and helped to entertain us, but the most fun were the good times in their own home, where music and youthful antics embellished every day.

I arrived back at the Institute in January 1926, expecting to continue in my luxurious leisure. But a letter from Ruth was awaiting me. She had taken sick and the doctor forbade her to continue with her physical culture class! "*Please* let father support you until I get stronger?" was her little wail. But I could not consider it: it was not in the "pattern" which God had showed me. *See that thou make all things according to the pattern showed to thee in the mount* (Heb. 8:5) was one of my lodestar verses: I must follow it.

From the mountain-top to the valley in one swing! How often life does just that. One moment having all things and at the peak of "fun"; the next moment facing a grim poverty and hard work. For I must seek employment now and I had lost the comfortable faculty waitress job—it was never available for me again. Totally unprepared for this, I had not been careful in my spending, and now I anxiously marshalled out my funds. Just enough to pay the first month's board money (we paid in advance) and with something like eleven or twelve dollars over. I'd barely make it. I must go to the Employment Office immediately and see what jobs they could find for me. Humanly speaking, the nicer jobs would be all gone by this time, and more than that—friends had been told that I was being supported through school and no one would think to send me any extra gifts! But the Lord had not left me; it was another chance to *search* His powers; He was just asking me to be willing for the uncongenial work again.

As I sat looking at my accounts I suddenly saw something that made me go cold. In the Christmas rush I had forgotten to tithe my last income! What should I do? Let the tithe continue to slide for a while? I pondered a moment. What came first in my life anyway? "Oh, Lord, You come first," I whispered and resolutely set aside the tithe. That left me less than two dollars for a month's car-fare and incidentals—and I still had no job.

Well, the Employment Bureau found me two; noon rush-hour girl at that same old restaurant, and waitress for Evening School supper at M.B.I. I was now very busy indeed. The long walk to and from the restaurant, a later hour getting to bed at night from the Evening School began to tell on my health. Always thin, it was dangerous for me to lose weight, but I knew that I was doing so. By February my friends were beginning to notice that I looked haggard and tired and I myself felt that I was near the breaking-point. "Lord, is it Thy will that I have a breakdown?" I prayed in private.

One evening I was called over to the Reception Room—a visitor for me. There, tall and smiling and fatherly, was Dr. Harrison! He was in the city on special speaking engagements and thought he would look me up. His keen eyes looked searchingly at me as we shook hands and he said, "How is it, Isobel? You look tired. Not working too hard, are you?"

"Perhaps I am," I answered. "When I returned here from your place I found that I must work my way again; the lady who had been supporting me since Marjorie stopped has been sick and can't do it any more."

"Well, Isobel," and the keen, kindly eyes again searched my face, "isn't it wonderful that *stop* isn't in the Lord's vocabulary? He never gets sick and He never forgets our needs and He is never at the end of His resources. Do you remember when you were at our place at Christmastime that you were invited out to dinner with Marjorie by a Miss Boyle?"

Oh, yes; that had been a real treat. Miss Boyle was a wealthy lady in Dr. Harrison's congregation. She lived in an exclusive apartment hotel, the kind of place where an ordinary mortal scarcely dared to look, leastwise enter. Because of her love for Marjorie, Miss Boyle had included me in the invitation, but she had scarcely noticed me beyond the usual courtesy care of one's guests. But I did not mind that; it left me free to enjoy the exquisite appointments of the room, the table and the meal. How much the Lord did give me! "As having nothing and yet possessing all things." I was beginning to understand what Paul meant. But Dr. Harrison was talking.

"I saw Miss Boyle just before I left and when she heard me say I was coming to speak at the Institute she said, 'Oh, by the way, I was thinking the other day that I have never donated anything to M.B.I. I feel I'd like to do so by way of that little friend of Marjorie's who came to my place for lunch that day.' And, Isobel, she handed me a cheque for two hundred dollars. I meant to give it you in small gifts, perhaps ten at a time. But maybe I'd better give it all to you now!"

Two hundred dollars—just like that. *At sundry times and in divers manners* truly!

"Oh if you did," I cried, "then I could give up one of my jobs and not have to work so hard."

"I'll see you get it tomorrow, dear," and that dear father-in-Israel went on his way.

So I was able to give up the evening work. The noon rush hour, though disagreeable, paid better for the time used, so I retained it. By this and the other gifts I managed to reach the summer.

When I returned for the last term (September-December

1926) I was once more faced with earning my way entirely, but I had left word with the Employment Bureau and they had tried to choose the best for me. For one thing, they had been in touch with Mrs. Allison of the Practical Work Department and she had given me a very special assignment for Sundays *which also paid a salary*! I was the Sunday pianist for St. Charles Reformatory for Boys; the Government paid for a pianist. I gasped at that assignment and straightway sought out Mrs. Allison.

"Oh, I can't play the piano well enough to hold down that job!" I expostulated. "I am largely self-taught, and always before this has been given to a music major student—isn't that so?"

"True," answered Mrs. Allison. "But I have heard you play for evening devotions and I think you can make it. I'll ask Miss X to give you some tips on evangelistic playing and get permission for you to practise on one of the pianos here. The reason I chose you is that there is such a wonderful opportunity there for personal work, and the lady who has been in charge up to now is sick. A friend is substituting for her, but is quite inexperienced in bringing children to decisions. You know the Reformatory, don't you? Every kind of boy problem is there, from playing hookey from school to murderers. There have been some wonderful conversions and we don't want to see it slump. You are paid to play for the morning and afternoon services, but you are *allowed* to visit the boys who are sick in the infirmary and deal personally with them between services. You get two meals into the bargain, so it will help you financially."

With fear and trembling I accepted, and for four months each Sunday was a thrilling experience. "My strength encampeth on weakness" is one rendering of 2 Cor. 12:9. The substitute leader who taught the Sunday school lesson in the morning service was very conscious of her inexperience and the pianist (!) trembled lest she be called on to give a piano solo, as sometimes happened. Truly we were weak, and therefore the Lord alone was exalted when scores of those boys decided for Christ. I could fill a chapter with all that took place at St. Charles

Reformatory; but this one happens to be on finances, so I must pass on and continue my theme.

Of course, Sunday piano-playing salary was only a mite. I had to take a major job besides that. The Employment Office felt they had a choice one for me. Again it was waitress (those hours fitted my schedule best), but at a very select tea-room near Michigan Boulevard. Noon and evening I was to serve and the salary promised was good. It was in a private house (one of Ruth's pretty, quaint tea-rooms) and the clientele were mostly high-salaried clerks or office-workers from the wealthy district around. Undoubtedly, I would get good tips in addition to the good salary. The proprietor was a widow, Mrs. Mac; the moral conditions had been investigated and all was trustworthy. Now at last I ought to have plenty of money; in one's graduation term one needed extras.

I liked it very much. Mrs. Mac was a middle-aged Southern lady, gracious and warm-hearted. The tea-room was pretty, the food delicious and the clientele were very nice to me. My tips grew. I was congratulating myself when a cloud appeared. At the end of the first month I walked in one morning to hear shouts and high words. The cook was swearing at Mrs. Mac, and the latter was at the phone.

"Isobel, stay here in this room," commanded Mrs. Mac, all flushed up. "This woman is threatening my life. I've called the police and I do not dare be left alone with her until they come here and put her out."

"No need for the police if you just give me my salary!" shouted the excited and irate cook. "This is a nice place for you to be in, Miss Isobel! She pays nobody! I've worked here two months and not got anything hardly. She owes the butcher, the baker, the . . ."

"Shut up," cried Mrs. Mac. "You lie. . . ." And then they were at it again when a tall policeman arrived at the door and the cook had to leave. My heart sank. That wonderful salary—would I really get it? Today was the end of the month. Just what was the situation, anyhow? Within a half-hour a new cook had arrived and the business of the day rushed on: but as I went from table to table my mind was also busy on this problem. Should I ask Mrs. Mac for my salary? Or should I just pray that God would move her to give it to me? By the end of the day I had made a decision—I would speak if she did not offer to settle accounts. She made no offer nor gave any hint that she remembered my salary was due.

"Mrs. Mac," I said as I put on my hat and coat. "Tomorrow is the first of the month and I must pay my board and room bill. Do you think you could let me have my salary tonight?"

She hesitated, then went slowly over to the till. "I had an unexpectedly big bill to pay today," she said. "Could you take just half now and I'll pay you the rest later?"

This was what I had feared; the dismissed cook had told the truth; Mrs. Mac was not in the habit of paying her bills. Her promises were wonderful, but it was quite a different thing to get her to keep them. Again I was in a predicament. If I told the Institute, they would recall me, of course, but at this late date what other jobs would be available? Here at least I got something from tips; in fact, my tips for the first month, combined with what she had just given me, made just about the sum of the promised salary, and this had given me an idea.

"Mrs. Mac," I said earnestly. "I am a Christian and accustomed to ask God directly for what I need. I cannot serve you for nothing; but I am willing to keep track of my tips, and at the end of each week if you will make up what is lacking to the amount of the salary you promised the Institute to give me, I will be content with that. Then we will just ask the Lord to move the clients to tip me as much as is needed."

She flushed a little. "But that is not right, Isobel. The tips should be yours as extra."

"But I am content and can make ends meet if I get what you originally promised me," I replied.

"It is very good of you," she said sadly, then opened up and told me her troubles. I do not believe she was deliberately crooked; she was just utterly undisciplined and improvident. She had no conscience about debt and spent freely what came in to the till. Each Saturday I faithfully reported my tips, which continued to be high, and as the weekly dole-out was not as high (she seemed to be better able to part with a small sum than a large one) she gave me her part. I believe now that I was the only worker she hired whom she paid regularly! Of course, I talked to her about trusting the Lord for her salvation. She liked to listen and often agreed with me, but that miracle of a new birth within her never took place; that I could see. I fear dishonest thinking had become a refuge from conscience with her. The new cook only lasted some six or eight weeks and then there was a scene similar to the first one. She would pay just a little bit on her big butcher's and grocery bills—just enough to keep the stores from suing her—but, of course, that could not go on for ever.

I believe it was December when one morning I walked in to find the tea-room empty—nothing cooking in the kitchen, nothing prepared for the lunch-hour clientele. I called Mrs. Mac, but there was no answer. The upper stories of this beautiful old home had been let out to roomers and one of them heard me and came downstairs, dressed for departure.

"There has been a big blow-up here," she said in a low voice. "I didn't get it all, but I think the old lady has gone bankrupt. The cook made a furore about salary not paid and Mrs. Mac said she wished she were dead. Do you think she can have hung herself in the cellar? Better go down and have a look. I'm going to my office. Goodbye." And I was left alone in the empty room.

There followed a nerve-racking experience. All was silent as the grave and imagination conjured up my going down a cellar and bumping into her dead body dangling from the rafters! I shook all over. I just couldn't get enough courage to open that cellar door and go down and look. I prayed for the courage to do so, but I did not receive it. I despised myself; I lectured myself; I asked the Lord how could I ever go to China if I did not have nerve enough to open a cellar door and go down and investigate? But I was petrified. I just could not do it.

At length after about an hour I heard a step on the verandah and ran forward eager to see another *alive* human being. It was Mrs. Mac.

"Oh, Isobel," she said with a heavy sigh. "I forgot about you. There won't be any more tea-room. I'm bankrupt and the receivers are coming to take over the building. I've lost everything. I couldn't stand the silence, so I've been out for a walk."

"Mrs. Mac, I do wish you would give yourself to the Lord!" and I tried again to help her, but nothing seemed to penetrate. She was appreciative, almost affectionate toward me; but in spiritual matters she was just vacant. She would not acknowledge she was a sinner and that is the first step toward knowing God: and so I had to leave her.

Again I was in a predicament—just a few weeks from graduation and no income! I remember only two details of those last days. Mother had left me her silver service and Father asked to buy it for fifty dollars—that helped a lot.

Then there was a day when a bill was due and I was five dollars short. I had been praying about it, but nothing had come in. The morning I had to pay it, I received a letter and in it was just five dollars. It was from an old Christian lady whom my father had visited, and when he told her I was working my way through Moody she decided to send me that gift. She had not given me anything before, and she never gave me anything afterwards; but the morning of my lack her five dollars arrived.

At sundry times and in divers manners, always the good hand of my God was upon me. He had wrought wonderfully for Hudson Taylor; but as I looked back over my two years and four months at the Institute I felt He had done just as wonderful things for little unknown Moody student me. *By searching* I had found Him able and faithful to supply my financial needs. And He will do so for any of His children who trust and obey.

CHAPTER ELEVEN

GRADUATION AND C.I.M. CANDIDATURE

I FINISHED at the Moody Bible Institute in December
1926, and I was elected as the girl class speaker (M.B.I. custom
demanded two valedictorians, one from the women's side and
one from the men's).

As I prayed for a message, thinking of our class as they would
be going out into the world to represent the Christ, I was given
the verse John 20:25 and took as my theme, *The Print of the
Nail*. I chose Thomas's words: "Except I shall see in His hands
the print of the nails and thrust my hand into His side, I will not
believe," and I made it representative of what the unbelieving
world is unconsciously saying to the Christian Church today.
The heathen around us have not much respect or interest in a
smug, ordinary Christianity. "If it costs you nothing, what proof
have you that it has any value?" is their indifferent, shrugging
attitude. But when they see in any life *the print of the nail*, they
are challenged; and like Thomas of old, if they can be made
to see Him at that moment, they will fall down and cry, *My Lord
and my God*.

I felt this message deeply and wanted it to speak to other
hearts as it had to my own. But M.B.I. required that the vale-
dictory messages be memorized (they had, of course, to be
careful that students represented correctly the teaching of the
Institute). This bothered me a little. The memory work didn't,
but I had never been able to pour out my heart unless given the
freedom of extemporaneous wording. I did not know this then,
for I had done comparatively little public speaking. I just knew
that I felt hampered, somehow, at reciting a memorized text.
But rules were rules and I fell in line, as I had tried to do
throughout the Institute days.

My father came to Chicago for my graduation, and Miss Boyle
sent me a white silk dress. She and I did not correspond; in fact,

apart from the two hundred dollar gift at the beginning of that year, I had heard nothing from her. And certainly no one was told that I had no money to buy the required white dress for graduation! (Remember, I had lost my employment at Mrs. Mac's.) Moreover, in those days M.B.I. required that girl students' clothing have sleeves below the elbow and skirts nine inches from the floor! The 1926 year styles were worn shorter than that, yet when Miss Jackson measured the gift dress it fulfilled all requirements and did not have to be altered at all. (Miss Boyle's gifts to me ended here. I've never heard from her since.)

As we went up to the platform, I, on sudden impulse, gave the text of my message to Anne Barr, our Vice-President, just in case I got stage fright and needed prompting. (I had recited the whole thing more than once before Mr. Bitticofer, so it was not that I did not know it.) When my name was called, I went forward and found that big audience. I did not feel as nervous as I expected and started in easily. But as I proceeded I felt that I was merely reciting, and not pouring out my soul; I found it was not going into their hearts and in my anxiety to give it the meaning it had for me, I forgot how the next paragraph started. It was only for a second and Anne behind me prompted quickly in a low voice that not everybody heard, but to me it was a catastrophe. I got through, went to my seat, hung my head and just waited until the end of the programme when I would be free to dash for my bedroom. Once up there (during my last term I had a room to myself), I fell on my knees in an agony of humiliation and failure. A pale December sun shone weakly through the heavy city atmosphere upon me, and then suddenly the Lord was there with me. I felt His love folding me around. "Never mind, dear," He was saying. "Failure or success it is all over now and My love is just the same."

"*The beloved of the Lord shall dwell in safety by Him; and the Lord shall cover him all the day long, and he shall dwell between His shoulders*" (Deut. 33:12).

The words were as if spoken, and the tenderness that engulfed me was balm of Gilead to my agonized soul. Slowly I quieted, relaxed, rested back on Him and drank deeply of His love. It was a wonderful experience and I was lifted up in spirit so that I no longer cared for any personal humiliation. I was deeply sorry I had disappointed the expectations of my class, but apart from that *I was beyond hurt*. I have never forgotten the outpouring of His love upon me that day when I felt such a failure.

After graduation came candidature at the China Inland Mission Toronto Home. Their yearly candidates' class had been in August, when Kathryn Kuhn and her brother John, with many others, had been accepted, and they had sailed for China that October (1926). I was the only candidate applying in mid-winter, and as I would be leaving for my home on the west coast, the Mission decided that I should come to Toronto immediately after graduation. As I was born in Toronto, we had relatives and friends there with whom my father stayed, waiting until he and I could travel west together.

Daddy Page came to the train to see us off. I do not know whether I was looking anxious or sad or just plain tired, but suddenly a tender compassion lit up his face and he leaned forward and said to me, "Don't be afraid, Isobel. There is nothing to dread in candidates' school. The C.I.M. has known you from a child." I thanked him for this good cheer and for all his loving, fatherly care of me during my Institute days, and then the train pulled out.

Mr. and Mrs. Brownlee were in charge of the Toronto Mission Home, but Mr. Seaman (the Seamans were on furlough and staying at the Home) was the one appointed to start me on the Chinese language study. Candidates learned to recognize the difficult radicals (roughly corresponding to the English alphabet and other sample beginnings). I was also to help and act as companion to the widow of one of the Mission donors; her bereavement had made her distraught and her family felt the quiet, prayerful atmosphere of the C.I.M. Home might benefit her.

The Brownlees' son, Dana, was present, otherwise the only other young person I remember was Ida McInnes. I had met Ida at Moody (indeed, it was she who had organized Daddy Page's surprise birthday party and had introduced me to John) and

learned to love her. She had graduated earlier and applied to the
C.I.M., but did not pass the medical examination. China being
closed to her, she became office worker for the Mission to Lepers
but was allowed to stay on in the C.I.M. Home until she could
find a boarding-house elsewhere.

Ida was "the embroidery" to my candidate days. She was
devoted to the Lord, and we were one in the things of the Spirit;
but next to that her keen sense of humour was a safety valve for
my youthful spirits. Quick, impulsive and day-dreaming, I had
been an easy prey to *faux pas* all my life and I was not in the
Home twenty-four hours before I had made the first one.

Knowing the Brownlees' reputation for perfect administration
I am sure the fault was mine, but I did not know the daily schedule.
Likely they had told me while I was day-dreaming! Conscious
that this was more than likely, I felt shy to ask what the hours
were, and decided to watch carefully the bells which summoned
the household to meals and meetings. I got along well the first
morning, but at 1.30 p.m. I was startled by a new clang. What
did that call me to? I rushed to Ida's room, but she was out. A
girl was dusting the corridor, so I asked her: "What was the
bell for, please?"

She looked at me wonderingly, "It's the prayer meeting
bell," she announced.

A prayer meeting? And the candidate not attending? That
would look bad.

"Sorry," I said hastily. "I'm new here. Which room is it?"

She told me, indicating the office buildings, and I rushed over.
The door was shut, but a murmur of voices within settled it for
me. I knocked gently and opened it. In my excitement, I did
not notice that only the staff was present!

"Excuse me for being late," I murmured and sank into a seat.
They received me politely, albeit a little blankly, and that day
the staff prayers were very general! After the meeting Mrs.
Brownlee came to me and told me gently that the 1.30 p.m.
meeting was for the staff only and that my presence would not
be required!

How Ida laughed when I told her. "They probably *discuss
you* at that meeting!" she teased, and from then on there were

many pointed remarks as to when my presence was required and when it wasn't! We had hilarious times in her room.

I was there some three or four weeks, and then I had to meet the Council. That is a formidable occasion and I was nervous, as I am not quick at thinking on my feet. I always do better with preparation and time to consider the best answer. However, the meeting came and went one afternoon and that evening after supper I was called in to the sitting-room by Mr. Brownlee to hear the verdict. He said something like this:

"The Council was quite satisfied with your answers today, and we in the Home have enjoyed your presence. But the Council has asked me to speak to you upon a very serious matter. Among your referees there was one who did *not* recommend you. The reason given was that you are proud, disobedient and likely to be a trouble maker. This person has known you for some years and the Council felt they could not ignore the criticism."

"Who was it?" I asked quickly, simply dumbfounded.

"The C.I.M. does not betray the confidence of referees. We write to those who have had business associations with you as well as to the referees you yourself give—and we promise to keep all reports in confidence. I cannot tell you the name, but I would like to discuss with you what havoc such characteristics can cause on the field." He then proceeded to do so. At the end of an hour of earnest exhortation, he pronounced the verdict: "The Council decided to accept you conditionally. There is an anti-foreign uprising in China just now which is very serious and we dare not send out any new candidates. That will be our public statement on this matter. For yourself alone, and we hope you will not spread it around, during your waiting period the Vancouver Council will be watching to see if any of these characteristics show themselves. If you prove that you have conquered them, you will then meet with the Western Council and be accepted fully, and sent out with the first party that goes. As we anticipate your victory in these matters, it was voted to pay your train fare to Vancouver, as *en route* for China. I can assure you I have not found it easy to say these things." And indeed his face was sad and tired. I felt sorry for him, even with the misery that was numbing my own heart.

"Good night." And I went up to bed, but, as you can readily believe, not to sleep. Who could the unknown referee be?

Proud. Disobedient. A trouble maker. This was the third time the adjective proud had been attached to me. The first time was by Daddy Page himself months ago: he had read me an anxious lecture on the subject, to my extreme surprise, for pride was one of the human frailties of which I felt I was not guilty. I would have taken Daddy Page's lecture to heart if he had not ended it by holding up to me, as one example to emulate, a certain fellow-student. That particular student stood high in the regard of the staff, but I happened to room near her and I knew that secretly she broke many Institute rules; also she lied about her age to her boy-friends, and so on. I was sure if Dr. Page knew what I knew, he would never have held her up to me as a pattern of conduct. So I concluded he just did not know either of us and brushed the accusation aside. China was later to be a painful revelation to me of my own heart and frailty. From this distance I now know that Dr. Page had indeed sensed a real flaw in my life; he had just got hold of the wrong label, that was all.

I was selfish. I had whimsically divided the world into two classes, people who interested me and people who did not. I felt I was not proud, because the people who interested me were often among the poor or the uneducated, but when it was so, my friendship for them was still as warm as for those who had had advantages.

Towards the people who did not interest me, I must have appeared proud. I cold-shouldered them and brushed them off me as time-wasters. This, of course, was a serious flaw for a missionary, but I fancy its basis was selfishness rather than pride.

The next point was—disobedience. How I did get indignant! M.B.I. had had many rules which were difficult to keep (they have since revised them, and it is no longer so), but I had been meticulous in obeying simply because I had signed a promise to do so, and I felt honour bound to keep it. Just the little matter of laundry, for instance. We had washbowls in our bedroom, but their use for laundry was forbidden—one pair of stockings a day was allowed, no more. Ransom Hall had then no laundry-room: I had to waste many weary steps going to another dormitory to do my laundry and waste more minutes because it was required that each time I get permission from the Matron to do so!—and I could not always find her. This was my most galling trial. The girl who had been held up to me as an example washed all her lingerie and sometimes even night clothes right in her bedroom at hours when she knew the inspectors would be busy elsewhere, and dried them on her radiator! "The rule is unreasonable" was her only answer when I remarked on it. But I had *promised to obey*, and so I dragged my weary self over to the other building every week. And now the C.I.M. had been told I was disobedient!

I had been told not to spread around this second condition of my acceptance by the C.I.M., but I did write a few friends. They wrote back quickly, indignant and sympathetic, and I was somewhat mollified. All but one. That one was Roy Bancroft, a music student with a beautiful baritone voice and a conse-crated heart. We had asked Roy out to St. Charles Reformatory to sing to the boys there and to help deal with them. I happened to be writing to him those days and impulsively told him. A letter came back quickly and I opened it with a smile of antici-pation, thinking that Roy too would be indignant on my behalf. But I got a shock.

"Isobel," he wrote, "What surprised me most of all *was your attitude in this matter*. You sound bitter and resentful. Why, if anyone had said to me, 'Roy B. you are proud, disobedient and a trouble maker,' I would answer: 'Amen, brother! And even then you haven't said the half of it!' What good thing is there in any of us, anyway? We only have victory over these things as we bring them one by one to the Cross and ask our Lord to crucify it for us."

These words "stabbed my spirit broad awake." Faithful friend he was, not afraid to *season his words with salt* even as he did not forget to speak *with grace* also: I was on my knees in no time asking the Lord to forgive me.

I arose from my knees with a different attitude. Instead of resentment there was alertness to watch and see if these three horrid "Diabolitians" (pride, disobedience, rebellion) were really lurking in my camp. The town of Mansoul should not protect them, if detected. This brought me into peace, even though I always shrank from the memory that I was to be watched for their appearance in my life.

Subsequently it so happened that in a most unexpected way I learned of my detractor's identity and then I knew the reason for her hostility. It will suffice here to say that she was a teacher in a school which I had attended. She wished me to assist her in spying on my fellow-pupils. I felt that was unworthy and so had incurred her displeasure by refusing. When I learned this I was tempted to clear myself with Mr. Brownlee and the Western Council. But should I? I seemed to hear a voice say: "If that had been said of me, I'd have answered 'Amen, Brother! And then you haven't told the half of it!' " Dear old Roy—he was right. Why try to make the Mission think I was lily-white? They'd have personal experience before long as to just how earthly a person I was!

"No Lord!" I whispered. "I won't bother the Mission with it. But how princely of You to let me know—it is like a miracle. Only You could have done it."

> For the Lord is always kind
> Be not blind.

Kind? To let me end up at Moody, where I had striven so to be faithful, under such a cloud? To let me begin with the C.I.M. under such a stigma? *Kind?*

Yes. You see, the Lord foreknew there was a work to be done in Vancouver before I sailed for China, and if I had ended up Institute life with great *éclat* I would quite possibly have wrecked that work at the very outset. My *self-confidence* needed to be thoroughly jarred before He dare put this delicate affair into my hands. And He had jarred it all right. My Master is thorough, "no one worketh like Him." But He had also been meticulously kind—just as soon as He dared, He had showed me why. And that after-graduation ceremony experience of His enfolding love has blessed me all my life.

Only *by searching* can we find out what He is.

Again to jump ahead of my story, but to complete this little matter, when the door did open for China again, Mr. Thomson wrote me a letter. I cannot quote it verbatim, but it ran like this: "I have never mentioned to you that little condition of the Toronto Council. From the first, both Professor Ellis and I felt there was a mistake somewhere, and I want you to know that so thorough was our confidence in this that I have not felt it even necessary to call the Western Council together. I phoned each one of them, and we all want you to know that you are accepted by the C.I.M. *unconditionally and unanimously*. Every one of them said that. And our loving prayers and blessings go with you."

I bowed my head over that little letter and wept tears of gratitude. Yes, my Master is thorough. He wounds, but He *binds up*, and His balm of Gilead heals without stinging; it cools, refreshes and restores in every part. He gives the garment of praise for the spirit of heaviness, and brings beauty out of our ashes.

CHAPTER TWELVE

THE VANCOUVER GIRLS CORNER CLUB

FATHER and I travelled on the train together from Toronto to Vancouver, and there my brother, Murray, met us at the station. It was strange to be together without Mother, and still stranger to find myself going across the ferry to North Vancouver in order to get *home*.

Father and Murray had rented a small four-room bungalow on Twelfth Avenue. Dad had one bedroom, I was given the other, and Murray put up a cot in the sitting-room at night and slept there. The fourth room was the kitchen; a bathroom separated the two small bedrooms, and a good big basement took in my trunk and suitcases. We three just barely fitted in the little place. Inside was more familiar, for there was Mother's piano, the well-known parlour chairs, equally familiar bookcases and a big fireplace—just like the one we had had in the old home. It was good to be back and I came to love that little house on the hill. From the front porch I could see the Harbour and the waters of Puget Sound, beyond which lay—China.

There now faced me the need for employment. I must earn my living until the door to China reopened. Was I to go back to school teaching? I would have to sign a contract and then would not be free to leave if the way opened before the contract date expired. I felt great reluctance in my spirit to do this. God had led me *out* of school teaching. I felt it would be like sending Abraham back to Ur of the Chaldees to return to it. While I was praying and pondering I received an invitation to speak to the Vancouver Girls Corner Club (V.G.C.C.) at their evangelistic service on the next Tuesday night. Yes, I replied; I would be very pleased to be their speaker; then, on leaving the phone, I asked my father who the V.G.C.C. were?

"Christian business girls banded together to try to win other business girls to the Lord," answered Father. "The Club was founded by Mrs. Neff, lady worker in the big French E. Oliver evangelistic campaign held here when you were in your teens. Don't you remember? Well, when the meetings were over they had a final supper with the converts, and some of the business girls got into a corner to discuss how they could keep together and keep going on after the campaign ended. They decided to form a club and to hold a weekly meeting to bring in unsaved friends. 'Here we are in a corner,' said one jokingly. 'Let's call it the *Corner Club*.' And that is how it started and how it got it's name. It's a fine work. I am glad you are going to speak to them."

The next Tuesday evening Father took me downtown to the Club rooms. They had a big lounge overlooking Granville Street (one of the busiest streets of the city), a small office for their Superintendent, and a big dining-hall where we went for supper. On Tuesday evenings a good supper was furnished for only fifteen cents a person; the dessert was always cake, and these delicious cakes were baked and donated by the women's societies in various churches, thus enabling the supper price to be low.

After supper the tables were cleared, pushed back and the chairs arranged for the meeting. A platform and piano were at the end of the long room and a bright evangelistic service was conducted for an hour. Christian business girls themselves led this meeting, and it was an enjoyable time, I thought.

In less than a week I received a second phone call. It was from the girls' President of V.G.C.C., and she astounded me by an invitation to be their Superintendent! I had not noticed that the position was vacant, but apparently they had been without one for some time. "We feel shy to ask you to take it," said the President, "because we can't afford to pay you the salary you deserve, or even as much as we have paid in the past. Corner Club is run down a bit, having gone so long without a Superintendent. We can only give you eighty dollars a month to start with. As the work picks up we would hope to increase it, but your hours will not be heavy. You do not need to be in the office until 10 a.m. each day."

When I asked what were the duties of the Superintendent, she replied, "Well, to lead and direct the work. Every day at noon tea, coffee and milk are sold in the dining-room. Business girls bring their bag lunches there and enjoy getting hot drinks to go with them. You will circulate among these girls, get to know them and try to lead them to the Lord. Every Tuesday evening you will be in charge of the evangelistic service and will speak. The Corner Club has had to draw speakers from various churches in the city during this period without a Superintendent, and we would like to pay back our debt to them, so to speak, by having you speak at any of their young people's societies who invite you. This would also advertise the Club. And maybe you yourself will create some new activities. Remember, our motto is *The Other Girl*." I asked time to pray about it and a date was set for my answer.

Nothing else offered, and as I waited in prayer I felt the Lord wanted me to accept; and so it came about that I became Superintendent of the Vancouver Girls Corner Club for the year 1927 and the early part of 1928. I had stipulated that the moment the door to China opened, I should be free to resign and that was agreed upon.

I now entered upon a fascinating period of my life. Corner Club was run by a Girls' Board, a Women's Board (representatives from different churches and different denominations in the city), the Superintendent and a business manager.

The business manager was a godly middle-aged woman whom everyone called Mother Fitch. Mrs. Fitch was one of those energetic saints who are described as *full of good works*. She had not enjoyed higher education but she had been taught of the Spirit and she simply lived for the glory of God and the winning of souls. There was no big evangelistic effort in Vancouver but Mother Fitch had a hand in it somewhere. The city missions were enriched by her prayers and practical services. Realizing that God had not trained her for platform work, she humbly accepted any mundane service—cooking, serving or even scrubbing—and prayed it into a ministry of blessing. Every Sunday she went to the jails to preach and during the week she ran the kitchen department of the Corner Club. Needless to say, I found in her a kindred spirit, although she must have been more than twice my age. We were a queer-looking team, but always a united one.

The Girls' Board were elected by the members of the Club. I was only twenty-five years old by now, and most of the Girls' Board, I think, would have been a bit older than that, but our times together are among my happiest memories. I have always felt that my Corner Club girls were among the loveliest young women that God ever made. They were ready for any venture that would win souls, but they were also a very merry group, and the Club rooms resounded with laughter and gay banter in between the earnest prayer meetings and discussions.

I did not meet the Women's Board immediately, and Mother Fitch laid hold of me early in that first week with a warning.

"Isobel," she said, "I would like to suggest to you that you do away with the Women's Board. They are not spiritually-minded like the Girls' Board, and I think they may be a drag on you. I believe God has sent you here for a red-hot soul-winning campaign and I am behind you one hundred per cent. You preach and I will cook! I know my place. The Women's Board won't allow you to give a call to decision on Tuesday nights, and I'm afraid you will meet with other restrictions. It is true the Club does get support from their churches and they would cut it off if the Women's Board were removed, but I am willing to live by faith like Hudson Taylor, and I am sure you are too. I think you could talk the girls into agreeing, for they are anxious to give you a free hand to direct things as God leads you."

Now, this was the delicate affair I referred to previously. I was young, inexperienced, and the words *red-hot soul-winning campaign* thrilled my soul. To give up a salary and live like Hudson Taylor would be heroic—just the strongest kind of appeal to me at that period. It was many years yet before a quiet article in the C.I.M.'s private *News Bulletin* alerted me to the danger of *missionary heroics*. That article pointed out that just because a line of action is difficult, painful or dangerous does not necessarily prove that it is the will of God. As a very simple instance, a call for medicine comes in the middle of a missionary's meal. She jumps up and leaves her food half eaten and rushes off to answer. That may seem noble and sacrificial on the surface; in reality, it is foolish and harmful. Of course, I am not referring to life-and-death emergencies, when promptness is a duty. I mean an ordinary medical call. The messenger has probably dilly-dallied several times already and an extra ten minutes' wait until the nurse's needed nourishment is properly masticated will hurt no one. As I read the article, I recognized my own photo-graph with deep chagrin. I was not given to breaking up my meal period, but I had been guilty of other extremes of conduct. Some natures are more open to this temptation than others, and mine is one. So at this time of my youth, Mother Fitch's sugges-tion appealed to me as quite possibly the highest line of conduct. I was cautious, however, and told her we must pray much before doing anything so radical.

I believe it was that very evening when I met the President of the Women's Board. She was a warm-hearted Scottish lady who shook hands with me, giving me a hearty welcome to Corner Club. Then she added: "You are a candidate of the C.I.M., aren't you? I'm good friends with the Charles Thomsons, and he told me to keep an eye on you and let him know *how you got on here!*" And she beamed at me cordially, perfectly un-conscious that she had just brought a whip-lash down over my shoulders with a sting!

I never for a moment doubted that Mr. Thomson had be-trayed our secret to her. Charles Thomson was a godly Scots-man, the soul of honour and common sense. I was sure that Mrs. Mc—— did not know the full implication of what she had said, but I saw in a second that I was in no position to begin my Superintendent's career *by dismissing her!* Some gentler method must be found, and so the Lord used this "whip-lash" to guide me on to a better road. I told Mrs. Fitch that I felt we should go slowly and try what prayer could do first. She sighed, but never refused a challenge to pray. The day was to come when the President of the Women's Board would kneel beside me in the little office, and with tears thank God that He had brought me to Corner Club. And I (likewise with tears in my heart) thanked Him for keeping me from the precipitate action which would have wounded this dear life and hindered the accomplishment of His purposes.

As I gradually met with other members of the Women's Board I found a group of women very different in temperament, but gifted, reasonable and co-operative. They did ask that I issue no calls to come forward for decision; they felt that the business girls would prefer more decorum and dignity in the Tuesday night services than the usual "penitent form" method, but they too were desirous to see people converted.

God blessed the Tuesday night meetings in a quiet way. Not many made an open profession of Christ (which troubled me), but the attendance grew by leaps and bounds. No one knew how difficult I found those services. I was tormented by fear of stage fright again; of my mind going blank like it had during M.B.I. graduation ceremony. Many a Tuesday night as the girls were gaily putting out the hymnbooks I slipped down the corridor to the bathroom (the only place where I could be sure I'd not be seen) and, leaning up against the wall, cried to the Lord for the nerve to go back and on to that platform. But He never failed me: the stage fright never came back seriously, and gradually I began to count on His help and speaking grew easier.

Invitations to the churches began to come too. Finding that several of the girls had beautiful voices, I organized and trained a quartette (following the teaching I had received at M.B.I. in such). One of the younger members of the Women's Board had a bell-like contralto voice suited to sing bass, so the quartette represented both the Girls' and Women's Boards and was a real success. "Miss Miller and the Corner Club Quartette" began to get calls from all different denominations, and our opportunities to witness for the Lord multiplied. Often we took our suppers to Club and ate them before leaving as a team for the church of the evening. Then it was that the empty dining-room rang with laughter, for all four had a keen sense of humour and the relaxation from their office work prompted an ebullition of youthful spirits. But always the evening's work was brought before the Lord in earnest petition before we left. I began to see what a power a Christian Business Girls' Club could be. Through its interdenominational character, it was quietly reaching out and challenging young people's societies in many denominations throughout the city.

And even into the business life of the city there was an influence going out. A lawyer asked what had caused the change in the life of his stenographer and her answer had an effect on him. I saw more and more the wonderful potentialities of the work when first things were kept first. There have been corner clubs in other cities, but the temptation is to let them sink into merely social service efforts. Young life must have an outlet, and I soon saw that. So we had picnics, seaside corn-roasts, hikes on Saturday afternoon and in the winter we had a "Stunt Night"— girls only. This was one of the most hilarious evenings I ever spent. The stunts were all wholesome fun and revealed much brains and talent. I myself had opened it, dressed up as the cartoon version of an old maid schoolmarm, and I announced that the students of my boarding school were about to put on a programme for their relatives and friends. Most of the girls had never seen me lay aside the dignity of my office just for fun, and it tickled their fancy to find I could enjoy a joke as much as the next one. That "Stunt Night" broke the ice between me and a certain girl for whom I had been fishing in vain for weeks. It was only a short time afterward that she accepted the Lord in my office. But all our parties were threaded through with the love of Him and a deadly earnestness that others might find Him too. I think that is the secret. A merely social club helps nobody very much, for it does not offer any solution to the problems of life.

My noontime circulating among the lunchers was to me the most difficult part of my work. Always shy about meeting strangers, I also had this unfortunate background of having so fiercely resented personal work in my own earlier days, so that it made me timid to barge in on other lives. I always felt I was a failure in the noon contact side of the work. A gifted evangelist could no doubt have reaped a big harvest from those opportunities. But I made friends and had their confidence. The sins and temptations which gradually opened up to me were appalling and led us into many unexpected adventures. I will just take space for two.

Edith was a clever young girl who had come out from England to get work in Canada and she lived with an aunt while doing so. She met and fell in love with a young man, and we followed her joy through the day she appeared in the lunch-room with her new diamond ring to the time when she said goodbye to office work and invited us all to her wedding. She had her dress and trousseau, had resigned her job, the wedding day was set and the invitations had all been mailed. A night or so before the actual marriage her telephone rang. Edith heard a strange woman's voice on the wire.

"Is it true that you are to be married to Mr. So-and-So in two days?"

"Yes," answered Edith, wonderingly.

"I am very sorry, but I must tell you he is already married. I am his wife. I have our wedding certificate here."

Can you imagine the shock to that young English girl? The shame? The heartbreak, for she had given her love unreservedly. But you cannot imagine the worst. Her aunt, humiliated at having to cancel the wedding invitations, in a towering rage ordered her out of the house. She would have no such thing of shame under her roof, she said.

Edith out on the street, homeless, wild with grief and heartache—where could she go? Her church? They were her aunt's type; probably would have the same views. *Corner Club.* She crept in broken, distraught—then found herself clasped on Mother Fitch's broad bosom. Corner Club protected her, loved her, found her a home and *led her to the Lord.* She proved to be an exceptionally gifted girl, and it was only a year or two before she had earned enough money to go back to England, where her own mother still lived. It was a soul saved and a young life saved, as well.

The most exciting story perhaps was that of Faye ———. A knock on my office door came one afternoon and I opened it to see a fashionably dressed woman standing there.

"Miss Miller? May I have a word with you? I have been to your Club rooms several times and admire the work you do very much. And in my boarding-house there is a young girl who needs help. May I tell you?"

I led her into the lounge and we sat while she talked. "She is a nice young thing from the prairies. Her mother is a widow, I believe, and sent Faye to Vancouver to study to be a nurse. She is a pretty girl and seemed to have a lot of dates with young doctors, you know, and I guess she neglected her studies. Anyway she failed her year, is out of the hospital, has no money, and I'm just anxious that the temptations of a big city do not suck her under. Do you think your Corner Club could help her? I told her you were very nice, despite—ahem—your long hair, and—ahem—your long skirts"—this with an eye to each. The fashions in 1927 you remember had shrunk skirts until they barely reached the knees, and although I had shortened my dresses I still felt that modesty required that the knees be covered. My hair should be long for the China of those days, so I had never cut it.

I was much amused at her two "ahems," but boldly ignored this little difference of opinion between us, and answered, "We would certainly do anything we could to help her. We are not an employment agency, but . . ."

"But you do have dishes to wash and dry?" urged the lady. "I thought if you could employ her here it would give you a chance to talk to her and perhaps steady her.

"I will consult our business manager," I replied. "Leave me your telephone number and I will call you. We do have dishes to wash, but our help is voluntary; our budget does not allow of much paid labour."

Mother Fitch, of course, was enthusiastic about taking in another young life to influence for Christ and it was agreed to employ her for a week or so whilst we sought to get her regular employment. So Faye was brought to us.

She turned out to be a gay little chatterbox. Most of the time she was busy in the kitchen, of course, but there came an hour when I was able to have her alone in the office and presented the claims of the Lord Jesus for her heart and life. She listened with the tears running down her face and acquiesced in everything. When she had left Mother Fitch came in to inquire about the result.

"Well," I answered slowly, "I am not satisfied. She was

certainly touched and willing to follow me in prayer and accept Christ as her Saviour. She wept; but somehow I cannot believe she is born again. Something did not seem to click—if you know what I mean."

Although not an employment agency, and certainly not a "rescue work," still it was possible at Corner Club to announce to the girls that a certain one needed work and to ask that the members keep their eyes open for a suitable vacancy. This we did, and Faye was not with us long before a noon-hour girl named Helen came to my office.

"Do you suppose, Isobel," she said, "that this girl Faye would be willing to take a poorly paid job until something better turned up? My mother has had a stroke and is completely paralysed—cannot even turn in bed. I am only an office worker and cannot afford a trained nurse to care for her during the day while I am away. But Faye has had some training; I would give her her room and board and a little for pocket money, if she would come and care for Mother?"

We called Faye in, and she accepted. She would be free every evening and we urged her to come to our Tuesday supper and service, and said goodbye. As our life was full of unexpected cases, it was not possible to follow up Faye very closely.

Summer came, and I was to have two weeks' vacation, which I chose to spend at the Firs Conference, very naturally. It was just a few days before I was due to leave when I got a telephone call from Helen.

"Isobel, have you heard about Faye?" she asked.

"No, not a word," said I in alarm. "Please tell me."

"Well, she is in the hospital. She began to act and talk strangely here and one evening she had a sort of spell so that I called in a doctor. He sent her to her old hospital and now he says she is insane! I don't believe it myself. In fact, I think she is acting a part to get away from here. It was a bit quiet for her, I guess. I feel she's been accustomed to hit the pace, you know. Anyway, I wish you'd go and see her. Her doctor might believe you. He won't listen to me. Here is his name and telephone number."

I was staggered at this news, but promised to go and see her.

Helen hung up and I called the doctor's number. A crisp, professional voice answered.

"Doctor, this is Miss Miller, Superintendent of the Vancouver Girls Corner Club. I believe you are treating Faye —— ?"

"Yes," shortly.

"Well our Club is interested in Faye, and I have been asked to go and see her at the hospital if you . . ."

"It would do no good, Miss Miller," came the answer quickly. "She would not know you. She recognizes no one, and I've had to put her in Ward X. She is violent."

"Well, Doctor, the friends with whom she was staying feel that she is just acting a part. . . ."

An exclamation of anger stopped me. "Miss Miller, I have been a specialist in mental cases for —— years. Do you presume to tell me I cannot recognize insanity?" He was clearly insulted.

"No, Doctor. I beg your pardon. But for the sake of her friends could you not give me permission to visit Faye? My pronouncement would quiet them."

He gave an exclamation of impatience.

"All right. Be at the hospital on Saturday afternoon at 2 p.m. I'll give orders for you to be admitted," and down went his telephone.

So down went mine too. And up went my heart to the Lord.

"Now, O Lord, I'm in for it! I've got a new search on now. Can you control the high-strung bunch of nerves which is me, and enable me to face an insane person?"

I think that most people have a private horror, a "phobia," some one thing. Most women fear snakes. I've known a big strong man just about go to pieces at the news that *a rat* was near. One famous scholar of our generation admits to a phobia as regards insects. Now my own private fear has always been insanity. I don't like snakes or rats, but they do not set my nerves a-jingle like the word *insane*.

"Lord," I prayed, "when I felt I should go down into that cellar to see if Mrs. Mac had hung herself there, I asked You for the nerve to go *and I didn't get it*. Of course, You knew she wasn't there and that I did not need it. But still—can You nerve me to face insanity? Saturday afternoon will be my proving time."

I was to leave on Saturday night for the Firs: so I was all packed and ready for the train. Leaving my baggage at the Corner Club, I proceeded to the hospital at 2 p.m., and inquired for Ward X. It was in the basement. Across the corridor were heavy, locked doors and in front of them, at the side, was a desk with two nurses seated there. Above the doors were the silent words, *Ward X*. From behind the doors someone was singing a ragtime at the top of her lungs.

I went up to the nurses and said, "Please may I see the patient, Faye ——"

The nurses looked at one another. "I'm sorry," said the older. "It is against the rules. No one is allowed to see her."

"But I was told that I might, if I came at this hour." Again they exchanged glances, then the younger said to me, "She is violent. That is her singing now!" The youthful voice was rollicking on.

"Dr. —— told me he would give orders to let me in," I protested. That was a magic word. "Oh," they scrambled through some papers on the desk. "Yes; there is an order for a Miss Miller."

"I am Miss Miller."

"All right. Step this way."

The younger nurse took a big bunch of keys and opened the corridor door, ushering me into the corridor on the other side. Small cells lined this corridor on either hand and each door was locked. Each cell was beneath the ground, but had one iron-barred window high up near its ceiling, and level with the earth surface outside.

My heart was beating so violently I felt dizzy and sick, but before I knew what was going to happen the nurse had unlocked a cell, *pushed me in alone* and I heard her lock the door behind me!

Faye stood with her back to the door, looking up through the little barred window and shouting her song. She was in a dishevelled mess that it would not be kindness to describe. At the sound of the door key she whirled around like a wild animal about to spring on its prey, but as soon as she saw me, she went limp, blinked stupidly a moment, then said, "Miss Miller!"

"Yes, Faye dear," I answered. Going forward and taking her in my arms, I kissed her. "I've only just learned that you were sick. I've come to see you. Get into bed, dear, and then we can talk."

Like a lamb she climbed on to her cot and I sat at the foot of it, as there was no chair in the cell—nothing else in it but the iron bed. I talked about the Corner Club, trying to draw her memory back to quiet scenes and to the Lord. She answered each question intelligently and only once did she exhibit anything strange. I was telling her of some little Corner Club incident and said, "Mother Fitch—you remember who she is, Faye, don't you?"

"Yes," replied the young face on the pillow. Then there came an expression of cunning, "*And I know you*," she cried emphatically. I went cold all down my spine, but ignored it, continuing on in my quiet chit-chat. I told her to trust in the Lord and that I would write to her mother. Also that I was going on my vacation, but would come and see her as soon as I got back. I suppose I stayed about fifteen minutes. Then I knocked loudly on the door, hoping the nurse would hear. She came at length and I left—Faye still quietly lying in bed.

When I got back to the Corner Club I phoned the doctor. "Yes," he said. "Well, how did you get on?"

"She knew me immediately, Doctor, and called me by my name."

There was a staggered silence at the other end, then to himself: "Well, I'll be d——d." To me, "Miss Miller, please tell me exactly what happened, right from the first." After I had done so, he said:

"How soon can you visit her again?"

"I'm leaving in a few hours for my vacation, Doctor. I will be gone two weeks, but I will call you as soon as I return."

"You do that!" he said earnestly, and we hung up.

Of course, I felt that Helen must be right—Faye was playing a part for some reason. If I had known it was so important, I would have given up my vacation to attend her, of course, but I didn't. In my next telephone conversation with the doctor on

my return from the Firs he told me she had been sent to E——
Insane Asylum, which was outside Vancouver. He was quite
indifferent whether I visited her or not, saying, "This time she
won't know you," but he gave permission for a visit with her.

Viewing the matter after nearly thirty years have passed, and
after having had more than two decades of experience with
devil-worshipping mountain tribes, I am inclined to think it was
demon-possession. The Devil has hoodwinked educated America
into thinking he is a myth, and he is working havoc unrecog-
nized. My reason for believing this is twofold. First, I found that
the mere presence of a consecrated Christian in a demon-haunted
house was enough to force back those powers. My entrance into
that hospital cell brought with it the power of my Master and
the demon force was temporarily quelled. Second, that look of
cunning when she affirmed (unasked!) that she knew me, was the
very same that I have seen on the face of a demon-possessed
tribesgirl just before that demon was cast out: and the com-
pulsion to confess recognition is similar to what took place in
our Lord's day. But as Superintendent of the Corner Club, I
knew as yet nothing of these matters.

Now I felt I must visit Faye in the asylum. Again I was
terrified at the thought, but as God had taken care of me in the
hospital, He would surely help me in this second step. So one
afternoon found me arriving by bus at the famous institution
which I had never dreamed I would ever see.

It was a huge place several stories high, and as I approached the
large entrance, men patients behind the iron bars of a veranda
screamed out to me and thrust their arms through the bars as if
trying to reach me. Not very soothing to the nerves! Inside I was
ushered first into the office of the resident physician. He was a
young man, and as I advanced to his desk he exclaimed, "Why,
it is Miss Miller!" It was my turn to be astonished.

"Isobel Miller of Arts 22, U.B.C. (University of British
Columbia), isn't it?" he repeated, shaking hands cordially.

"Why, yes. But how on earth do you know?" I queried. He
laughed.

"I was an undergraduate, a year or so behind you. What have
you been doing since?"

And so we had a little chat. My work at the Corner Club brought up Faye. There must have been several thousand patients in that place, so I asked, "Would you know Faye ——?"

"Would I?" he returned. "I'll never forget the night they brought her here. It took four strong men to hold her!"

"What do you think? Is she incurable?"

"No-o," he answered thoughtfully. "This type is brought on by dissipation and with the use of modern drugs we can often effect a cure. Did she talk very much? That is the first sign it is coming on—extreme talkativeness. She'll be here two years at least, though, and then there is likely to be a recurrence later on."

"My Club would like to help. Of course, we believe that prayer will help her, but is there anything else you could suggest?"

"Yes," he answered. "She has got run down through late hours and the life she led. If your Club could send her nourishing food, extra protein values, meats and broths, etc., that might hasten recovery. The ordinary food here is good, but she needs extra meat and such, which a Government institution can hardly provide."

I promised that we would do our best, and he rang for an orderly to show me the way to Faye's ward.

"They must prepare her to see you," he warned, "so you will have to wait a while."

Again I was taken to a corridor with a locked door in it. But also a lounge-room opened off at the side where harmless patients were sitting around, some embroidering, some reading, one playing the piano, and a nurse at a desk was obviously in charge. A bench was opposite the locked door and I sat there to wait. Up tripped a young woman who asked me boldly, "Who have you come to see?"

"Faye ——" I replied, rather wonderingly.

"Oh yes, a nice girl, I know her!" This with a loud voice, with her eyes on the matron at the desk. Then behind her hand in a whisper to me: "She is no more insane than I am."

"I've brought her some chocolates. Do you think she'll like them?" I asked more to make conversation that anything else.

"Oh, yes. The food here is fine!" This in a loud voice toward the Matron, then behind her hand in a whisper, "It's awful. They starve us. Bring her *lots* of chocolates!" And so she went on—compliments in a loud shout Matron-ward, complaints in a whisper behind her hand to me. It was all I could do to keep my face straight, but evidently she was known to them, for after a few minutes the Matron quietly lifted her head and ordered, "K——, you come back in here."

"See our bondage!" whispered the woman, making a wry face to me, but she obeyed.

At length a nurse came with a key and I was again ushered in behind the door to where a second nurse had brought Faye, then (to my horror) both nurses left me alone and locked me in with the patient.

I would not have recognized Faye. She was so thin she was the mere shadow of herself. The "preparation" they had given her was to drug her into stupidity, then immerse her, hair and all, in a bath to clean her up. She stood before me swaying unsteadily, her damp hair clinging to her like a drowned rat's, and she obviously did not know me. I told her my name and she repeated it, but with no sign of recognition. I proferred the chocolates and she opened them eagerly, popping them into her mouth one after the other rapaciously. Within five minutes, I knew that conversation was useless. It was true, she did not know me nor could she follow my thoughts.

Then the effect of the drug began to wear off. She had been brought to me in a corridor, off both sides of which were rooms. "I want to go back!" she said suddenly, and started staggering down the corridor, hunting for her own room. As I did not know it, I knocked and banged on the locked door to call the nurses back. At length one came and took Faye to her place. But by this time Faye had evidently come to. She turned fiercely on the nurse, swore and cursed her. A glimpse into the room showed me why they had had to drug her and bathe her before allowing any other human being to see her. Obviously she was living like an animal. Heartsick, I turned away and came home. It was an experience I would not care to have often, but the Lord had strengthened me to go through with it.

At the Corner Club I did not describe the above; merely gave the doctor's advice to send her nourishing foods. I told how emaciated she was and asked for prayer. I also wrote to her mother and the result was that a sister was sent to Vancouver to visit Faye and care for her needs.

Prayer was made constantly for the poor child's recovery and cartons of jellied chicken, home broths, jellies and other good foods were sent by the girls and the Women's Board. Still we were not prepared for our dear Lord's *abundantly above.*

Within *six months* Faye was dismissed cured! After asking the Lord to do this daily, I was taken aback by His speed! I received a telephone call from a stranger one day which ran something like this: "Miss Miller, you do not know me, but I am Mrs. X——, neighbour to Faye ——'s mother on the prairies. My husband and I are on this trip to the coast and Mrs. —— asked me to bring Faye home with me when we return. You know she was dismissed from the hospital a few days ago? No? Well, she was. She is living with her sister, but would like to come in and see you before she leaves and thank you for what you have done for her. May I bring her this afternoon? We leave by the evening train. Thank you. At three o'clock, then."

I sat back in my swivel chair and gasped. Then bowed my head and thanked the Lord.

I awaited three o'clock with a little trepidation. I had met two very different Fayes already. Which one would this one resemble? The gay chatterbox? The doped animal? Could she really be normal? The third Faye was the real Faye and a distinctly different person still. She had gained weight to a pleasing plumpness, but she was so shy and quiet I could hardly recognize her. She thanked me prettily and sincerely, but when she was gone into the kitchen to salute Mother Fitch I turned to their neighbour and said, "My, she is quiet! Do you think she is afraid of me?"

The lady widened her eyes with astonishment. "Oh, no. Faye never did talk much. She was always the quiet one. She is just like she used to be. Her mother will be delighted."

And so we parted. But my story isn't ended.

Nine years passed and now I was back at Corner Club as a missionary on furlough, as a married woman and as a mother.

What a welcome they gave me! But before the first message, which they asked me to give at the old Tuesday evening hour, I had had a telephone call.

"Isobel, I wonder if you will remember me; Faye —— ?"

I nearly jumped out of my skin. "Faye! You back in Vancouver?"

"Yes. But I'm married now. Oh Isobel, the Lord has been so good to me. I want to tell you all about it before you meet my husband. Will you take supper with me downtown, just we two alone, and then I will go with you to the meeting. My husband is coming to the meeting tonight—I got permission to bring him, since John, another man, will also be present. But I want you to hear my story first."

I wonder if you can understand my joy? No one can who has not mothered spiritual children. No one can who has not stood and watched the brand blazing in the fire, and then shrunk from the heat which almost scorched the hand stretched out to snatch it from the burning!

That evening in a little cubby-hole of a restaurant we sat face to face once more. She was still sweet-faced Faye, her quiet manner lit up with heartfelt gratitude. "Yes; I have a good husband and two darling children. *And I've never had a recurrence.* I'm sure the Lord won't let me now. And, Isobel, I want my children to be brought up in the Church. My husband and I are agreed: we want a Christian home."

Just one little peach from a year's harvest at the Corner Club. What potentialities lie in such work—leading business girls to Christ.

Often, on furloughs, I have heard the impatient remark: "Why go to the foreign field? There is lots to be done at home here!" There most certainly is. And there are lots of Christians at home—are they doing it?

By searching for Him, He makes us conscious of the need of others, and helps us cut channels by which He may be poured into their lives. In no time we find ourselves His fellow workers, and life is rich.

But I must come back to my tale: for by now the door to China was opening again.

CHAPTER THIRTEEN

"LET US GO ON!"

IT was the spring of 1928 when the China Director of the C.I.M., Mr. Gibb, paid Vancouver a visit. I was called in to meet him and well remember the searching look of concern he gave me. "My dear girl," he said, "you look worn out. Are you well enough to go to China?"

"Oh, yes. Physically I am sound. But I am very tired," I admitted. Our home on the north side was so far away from the evening church appointments. Late at night the ferry did not run so frequently and if I just missed one there was a long wait before the next. Often it was midnight before I got to bed, and 6 a.m. was my rising hour if I was to have a quiet time, get the house chores done and catch the 9 a.m. ferry.

But I think most of it was emotional fatigue. Mentally I knew the way of victory. I had read of Hudson Taylor's experience, *The Exchanged Life*, when he rolled all his burdens on the Lord. I had heard Keswick teaching expounded at the Firs and seen it lived in lives there. But how to transmute it into experience was beyond me. I secretly worried about things. My father's Micawber-like attitude toward business appalled me. Where would he end up? Now I knew my mother's secret trial and how much we all owed to her sound judgment and carefulness.

I worried about my own failure at the Corner Club. I did not have the gift of evangelism. Young lives were constantly being cleansed, rededicated and built up in Him, but I did not see that. I looked just for souls to take the initial step of salvation. Pentecostal girls were urging me to seek the baptism of the Spirit. One of them was a gifted evangelist, a golden-haired, angel-faced girl, and I fell into the snare of comparing myself with others. Peggy had something I didn't. Was it really the speaking in tongues? Inwardly I fretted. But the Lord was carefully holding me. I asked Peggy and Dorothy (another who kept at me) to describe what happened when they were "filled with the Spirit." Their most vivid descriptions were no more than what I myself had often experienced when alone with Him and the awareness of His presence would flood in. I had never spoken in tongues, but I seemed to have had everything else they claimed to have experienced. This kept me.

I always felt there was a peril in just seeking an *experience* from the Lord. The temptation is to think *the experience* has sanctified. It hasn't. These uplifting times in His presence, provings of His faithful care, *enrich* us, add to our joy, but they do not sanctify us. They do not make us stronger Christians; they do not make us holier than our fellows, as I was to learn to my shame. But they make us richer in our knowledge of Him, and they give us joy that addeth no sorrow to it. The only way to be holy is daily to hand over to the Holy Spirit what Dr. Tozer calls "the hyphenated sins of the human spirit . . . self-righteousness, self-pity, self-confidence, self-admiration, self-love and a host of others like them . . . can be removed only in spiritual experience, never by mere instruction. As well try to instruct leprosy out of our system. There must be a work of God in destruction before we are free. *We must invite the Cross to do its deadly work within us. We must bring our self sins to the Cross for judgment.*"[1] The Holy Spirit will crucify these things for us, as we hand them over to Him, and then we must just accept the suffering involved, rejoicing in the knowledge that His resurrection life will be the final outcome.

And so with all my rich experience of answered prayers, I still was full of worry, self-pity and many other ugly things: but I was not acutely conscious they were there.

Mr. Gibb was really perturbed. By now I wore an engagement ring, and John Kuhn was already in China and being used of the Lord there. If my health broke, would that bring John home? He consulted Mr. Thomson, and they both ordered me to resign from the Corner Club and take six months' complete rest before sailing in October (1928). Mr. Gibb intended to give instructions that I be put on Mission remittance in order to do this, but, most

---

[1] *The Pursuit of God*, by A. W. Tozer.

unusually for him, he must have forgotten. I waited and waited, but the C.I.M. sent me nothing. And I felt I should not petition for it. Hudson Taylor would have just prayed.

I forgot how it happened, but Mr. and Mrs. Whipple heard of the order for me to rest and invited me to spend the five or six months at the Firs. I could help in cleaning cabins and getting the Conference grounds ready, but first I was to have a full month of just rest—breakfast in bed! and so on.

I had been able to save no money, for I had felt I should pay my father's debts. It was clear to me that the next invention would never bring him in an income, and I was right. So I landed at the Firs with about thirty-six dollars (I think it was), all the money I had left.

Maybe one reason my heart longed so for a home on the Crescent where I could give rest to tired business girls was due to my own experience. No one can know what it meant to me to be taken in by dear cheery Mrs. Whipple and be given the upstairs porch which they were fixing up as bedroom for their own daughter, Lois, when she should return from the Bible Institute of Los Angeles, where she was studying. Two sides of the room were without full walls and the scented, tall fir trees were its screen. Mrs. Whipple had procured some old cement sacks; she bleached them, stencilled a pretty fleur-de-lis pattern on them, and hung them up in lieu of walls. When Conference would bring many people around and the fir trees might not afford privacy enough, these could be drawn. But when I arrived the scented green needles were the wall, and I loved it. To wake up in the morning just when you had slept to the full, no pressure of schedule upon you, to hear the birds carolling and the sun trying to peep at you through the green foliage was like living with God in Eden. I can never forget it.

I knew that Whipples were "living by faith," but had no idea that when they took me in that first night they were down to rock bottom financially. I just felt I would like to give them my thirty-six dollars. Before going to bed, I handed it to her, saying: "I want you to take this. It won't pay for all I'll eat these months, but I'd feel happier if I felt I'd given something."

I remember Mrs. Whipple flushed a bit and tried to refuse,

but I insisted and then the matter left my mind. She told me years afterward that that was one of the hardest things she ever did—to take my money. But the milk bill was due in the morning and she had nothing else with which to meet it! And I myself would need milk. My money fed us until a gift of sixty dollars (I think it was) came in; and from then on there was no shortage. This is just a glimpse as to how the Whipples lived; although gifts had been few, they did not hesitate to invite me to live with them for six months! And I do not need to say how God blessed them.

They had returned from China to find that the Firs was the only home they had. With funds low and the need to make and furnish a bedroom for Lois (and me!), they were put on their mettle. From the attic of a relative they obtained some old furniture free, and this they sand-papered and repainted a pretty green for Lois' bedroom. When the stencilled curtains were hung, it was as dainty a room as a girl could wish—and I had learned lots about how to convert old things into new!

The Conference that summer (1928) was the most blessed I had ever known. The special speaker was Dr. Arthur Harris of Wales, and the Spirit of the Lord was powerfully among us. For one thing, Mrs. Whipple had prayed that every young person attending the Conference should yield to the Lord before going home. One evening during the service she was impelled to go to the girls' dormitory, and there she knelt by each bed, claiming for Christ the occupant of that bed! Needless to say, every evening there were decisions made. Toward the last evening there were a few who still hung back from full surrender, so the staff called us leaders of the young people to pray all during the evening service. I can never forget that prayer service. The Spirit of the Lord came down upon us as in apostolic times, and we all started to pray simultaneously out loud. As for myself, I was not even conscious of the others. So lifted up into the Lord's presence and so burdened for the souls that were hanging back, that it was not till a break came that I suddenly came down to earth and realized that we had all been praying out loud at the same time. From the upper room where we prayed, down through the tree tops, we could see the open-air auditorium. As we prayed, one after the other of the recalcitrant ones got up and went forward in surrender. The very last, a girl for whom I had had little hope, has now been for decades a most faithful missionary on a foreign field. Very truly it was the work of the Spirit of God.

Conference over, I needed to go back to Vancouver and get my outfit ready for China. There were still no funds sent to me by the C.I.M., but a love-gift from my brother paid my fare home. (As he, Murray, saw the invention was not likely to make Dad rich, he set about getting a job.) But where would the next come from? To add to the perplexity came a letter from Marjorie Harrison saying that she was travelling in our party and would like to stop off and see us! When I answered with a cordial invitation, I did not have enough money to pay her car-fare from the station to our home, let alone feed her.

Then I got a call from Mr. Thomson to come to his office, as there was some money waiting for me. "At last!" I said jubilantly to myself. Mr. Gibb has remembered his promise! But it was no such thing. It was much more wonderful than that. It was fifty dollars from my own dear John in China! I think it was the remainder of a bank account he had left over from his earnings in preparation for Moody. "I want to have a share in your outfit," he wrote, "but it has no strings on it: you may use it for any need." And the first bit of it fed Marjorie!

From then on I had no difficulty. Corner Club girls gave me "showers" and a beautiful outfit, which included the money to buy a portable organ! That little organ went with us to the Salween mountains and brought much joy to Lisu as well as missionary for many years: and it must still be there.

I prayed much about my final message at the Corner Club. I did not know (though I shrewdly suspected) that some of those dear girls were going to prove prayer warriors for whom I would thank the Lord all my missionary days. And it has been so now for twenty-eight years. God laid on my heart a message for myself as well as for them from Heb. 6:1, *Let us go on*. The search is not ended. We have only begun to explore our eternal unfathomable God. "Let us leave behind the elementary teaching about Christ and go forward to adult understanding.

Let us not lay over and over again the foundation truths. . . .
No, if God allows, *let us go on*," paraphrases Phillips. And that
was the burden of my message.

On October 11, 1928, I sailed for China. There was quite a large
party of us (one being the little American girl who roomed next
me in Ransom Hall at Moody. Ella Dieken was engaged now to
Jack Graham and we were to be room-mates at the Language
School in China). My father had got permission to sail with me
on our boat as far as Victoria so that the emotion of parting from
him did not take place at the Vancouver Wharf. It was about the
noon hour when the ship was due to pull out and the Corner Club
girls forgot their lunch and flocked down to the wharf. They
made such a crowd that a stranger asked my brother, "Who is
the girl who is getting this send-off?" Just an unknown missionary going out for the first time, was certainly not the answer
expected. But God can give special things to His unknown
children when He wants to.

At last a bugler climbed up to the highest bridge of the
Empress of Russia and began to play Queen Liliuokalani's
beautiful farewell song "Aloha Oe." It is, of course, the sad
parting of two lovers. It breathes passion, but no certitude of
hope. It is earth doing its best to reach out for cheer, but failing
mournfully. I am so glad that Christian words have been set to
it for such moments. For it is only Christians who dare to say,
"We never part for the *last* time." As the bugle notes poured
forth on the noisy air of the wharf, there gradually grew a
stillness over the crowd,

> In these the closing days of time
>   What peace this glorious thought affords
> That soon, O wondrous truth sublime,
>   He shall come, King of Kings and Lord of Lords.
>
> He's coming soon, He's coming soon
>   With joy we'll welcome His returning
> It may be morn, it may be night or noon
>   But oh, He's coming soon.

But "the gospel must first be published among all nations"
(Mark 13:10).

And we, who living yet remain
   Caught up shall meet our faithful Lord.
This hope we cherish not in vain
   But we comfort one another with this word.

The last notes quavered sadly on the high air. The unbelieving in the crowd, grasping the only best they knew, whispered, "Aloha Oe." The big anchors rattled as they were pulled up, the paper streamers began to tear as the mighty ship slowly drew away from the wharf. Beloved girl faces were working with emotion, and one or two were crying. "Lord," I whispered, "give me a last word they won't forget." A thrown voice could still reach the wharf. I leaned over the side and called out slowly, *"Let us go on!"*

The light of heaven broke through the tears of earth on some faces, so I knew they had heard. They waved their hands in a signal of assent and then the *Empress of Russia* turned her stately head slowly toward the Narrows, Puget Sound, the Pacific Ocean and—China.

But there was one more step. At the city of Victoria, on Vancouver Island, my father said goodbye and disembarked. After he had left, the purser brought me a telegram. It read simply, "WE WILL GO ON—YOUR CORNER CLUB GIRLS."

Tears of gratitude rained in my heart. Twenty-eight years have passed—a good, long testing period? Corner Club is still operating. Most of those girls have gone on. There are people in more than one country of the world who rise up and call some of them blessed. One of them on the wharf that day had unconsciously been leaning on me rather than on the Lord Himself, so she sprawled spiritually when her human prop was removed. But on the whole they kept their promise.

And now, as reader and author part, I can find no better words to use than just these same, *"Let us go on."* Go on searching and exploring the greatness and the dearness of our God.

He has no favourites. He has said, "Ye shall find me when ye shall search for me with all your heart" (Jer. 29:13).

Notice that last phrase, for it is the only condition. There must be inner honesty and undivided loyalty—that is the only stipulation. "The man who trusts God, *but with inward reservations*, is like a wave of the sea, carried forward by the wind one moment and driven back the next. That sort of man cannot hope to receive anything from God, and the life of a man *of divided loyalty* will reveal instability at every turn" (Jas. 1:6-8—Phillips thus paraphrases it).

But—"He is a rewarder of them that diligently seek Him" (Heb. 11:6).

Said Susanna Wesley, "He is so infinitely blessed, that every perception of His blissful presence imparts a gladness to the heart. Every degree of approach to Him is, in the same proportion, a degree of happiness."

So—*Let us go on*—SEARCHING.